MW00697274

# You've Got To Be HUNGRY!

*The GREATNESS Within to Win*

Please join my online community by visiting www.iamhungrylesbrown.com or scanning the QR code above By registering, you will have access to private video messages, self-development exercises, exclusive file downloads, first opportunity to purchase new products and register for upcoming speaking engagements, as well as many other amazing benefits and opportunities. Hope to see you there!

For More information and more resources you can connect with us further at the following locations:
Coaching@iamhungrylesbrown.com
Corporatetraining@iamhungrylesbrown.com
Funding@iamhungrylesbrown.com
Credit@iamhungrylesbrown.com
Publishabook@iamhungrylesbrown.com
Franchise@iamhungrylesbrown.com

## *The Greatness Within to Win*

Copyright © 2019 by Les C. Brown

ISBN: 978-1-7327450-2-5

Scriptures marked KJV are taken from the King James Version (KJV): King James Version, public domain.

Scripture taken from the New King James Version. Copyright © 1982 by Thomas Nelson, Inc. Used by permission. All rights reserved.

All rights reserved. No part of this book may be reproduced or used in any manner without the written permission of the copyright owner except for the use of quotations in a book review. For more information use contact below:

Published by Brown Family Publishing
info@BrownFamilyPublishing.com
www.iamhungrylesbrown.com

# You've Got to be HUNGRY

# You've Got To Be HUNGRY!

## The GrEATNESS Within to Win

### by Les Brown

*The World's Leading Transformational Voice*

Published by Brown Family Publishing

info@BrownFamilyPublishing.com

www.iamhungrylesbrown.com

# Dedication Page

I dedicate this book to both of my mothers. To the one who gave me life, and to the one who gave me love.

I am grateful to God, who took me out of my biological mother's womb and placed me into my adoptive mother's heart. I truly feel Like Abraham Lincoln in that all that I am, and all that I hope to be- I owe to my mothers.

I also dedicate this book to all foster and adoptive children and their parents throughout the world. To the parents- thank you for your love of children who need it most.

To my children- I love you and appreciate your contribution to my life. You are my legacy.

I am also grateful for and dedicate this book to all of my spiritual sons and daughters around the world. Thank you for allowing my messages to penetrate your heart.

# *The Greatness Within to Win*

Of course, this is dedicated to entrepreneurs- and to every person who is hungry to live a life that will outlive you!

To the speakers and trainers that I have worked with and coached- thank you for entrusting me with one of your greatest assets- YOUR VOICE!

To everyone who religiously watches me on YouTube, follows me on social media, and has heard and allowed my voice to expand your vision of yourself, touch your heart, and unleash the greatness in you to make a difference in your lives- I dedicate this to all of you.

You are the hungry ones.

I know that this book will contribute to your journey as you manifest your greatness!

# Acknowledgments

This book would not have been possible without the collective insight and collaboration of some of the greatest minds around- who just so happen to be some of the people closest to me!

I am forever indebted to my family, friends, and business partners who contributed to this work in invaluable ways. I consider this to be my greatest work and I am grateful for your advice, patience, and persistence, as well as your contribution in helping me to complete this project.

Thank you to:

My daughter, Dr. Ona Brown- you have rightfully earned the title that you've held for years. You truly are "The Message Midwife" and I am humbled by your genius. Thank you for working feverishly around the clock to see that this work was birthed in the voice that is authentic and true to all that I represent.

## *The Greatness Within to Win*

Laneen Haniah, who was able to quickly, skillfully, and uniquely capture my voice and the spirit of my plight to change the world. I appreciate your gift.

Odeidra Williams and her company, Insight Write- thank you for seeing my vision.

Celeste Jonson, who once traveled with me as my assistant and has now evolved into her own nationally and internationally known brand because of her powerful speaking and singing voice.

Shaune Arnold, who like me was a foster child and is now my personal attorney and brilliant mind who inspires wherever she goes.

Terry Leggins, who teaches people how to write their story. Thank you for working closely with me to tell mine.

Dwight Pledger and Dan Smith, who taught me the art of three-dimensional storytelling which has given me the ability to orchestrate an experience that transforms people's lives both individually and collectively.

## *You've Got to be HUNGRY*

My childhood friend, Dr. Anthony Sweeting, a prolific writer, great speaker, and author. Thank you for always being there with me.

My long time mentor, friend, strategist, and surrogate father- Mike Williams, the author of the book, "The Road to Your Best Stuff." Thank you for seeing the Les Brown who I am today, long before I did. For over fifty years, you've honored your commitment to my mother, who said to you, "Take care of my boy." You've done that and more.

Finally, to all of my children- I know it has not been easy having to share me with the world. Thank you for your patience and understanding with me throughout all of the years. I hope you each know how much you mean to me. You were always my WHY.

There are no words to adequately express how fortunate I am to call myself your father and I am eternally grateful to your mothers for raising you to be incredible adults. You all have your own powerful and amazing stories that the world is awaiting. Thank you for the gifts that you are and for giving me my beautiful and especially made grandchildren and great-grandchildren.

# Foreword

Les Brown is one of the world's leading keynote speakers. He's been heard by billions of people and he truly is one of the greatest motivational speakers of all time. I realize that is a strong statement, but I believe it wholeheartedly.

Growing up I was a very shy kid. Les Brown was a major source of encouragement and motivation for me. I used to watch him and listen to his audiotapes. His words were incredibly inspiring. When I had the first opportunity to meet Les Brown, in 1991, it had a significant impact on my life. I was brand-new at running my own business and my encounter with him contributed greatly to my impending success. As destiny would have it, twenty-five years later I found myself speaking on a panel with my mentor, the one and only Les Brown. I never would have imagined it!

Suffice it to say, I've had a long history with Les. In my opinion, everyone can benefit from listening to him, no matter where you are in business or life. Whether you just need some general guidance on success principles, or you are feeling down and out, unmotivated, and scared – Les Brown has a word that will help push you to greatness! Not only is Les one of the greatest mentors you can have, he has also been through and overcome immense adversities.

In this book, you will walk through Les's transformation from growing up in a poor section of Miami to becoming one of the world's leading motivational speakers. Although many of the stories in this book have been shared before, they have never been presented the way they are in this life-transforming manuscript. This book is less like reading and more like having the experience with him! You'll also read about something Les has NEVER shared before. When you get to Chapter Eight, "The Story Never Told", you'll read for the first time ever about Les's addiction to prescription painkillers.

The story is absolutely soul-shaking, but I won't give away the details here. I'll let you read it for yourself. I will tell you this, in Mr. Brown's own words: "The detoxification process was worse than a living hell!"

During that time, Les reached out to me and I was able to help guide him through that dark phase of his life. You see, even though I found success in business, I was at one time an active and struggling addict who had to overcome many personal demons myself. I understood exactly what Les was going through. In a lot of ways, things came full circle; Les was able to help me earlier in my life, and then later in life I was able to help him.

I spend about half of my time utilizing my marketing skills to help people who struggle with addiction. I do this through my 501(c)(3), Genius Recovery. The goal of Genius Recovery is to change the global conversation concerning people with additions — changing the tone and perception from one of judgment to one of compassion. I want to change how people view and treat addicts and find the best forms of treatment that have efficacy and then share those treatments with others.

When Les asked me to write the foreword for his new and greatest work, *You've Got To Be HUNGRY*, I was honored. I plan to give this book to the people I reach in the recovery world. Doing recovery work – whether it's a 12- step approach, therapy, yoga, or anything else – is only one part of the process. Filling your mind with positive, motivational encouragement is another process entirely, and an essential part of recovery and sustainability. Les Brown's material is some of the best out there to aide in this process, and his new book will be a powerful addition to any motivational arsenal.

Les is great at not only helping people tackle lack of motivation or lack of clarity in their lives, but also helping people overcome personal demons. I see Les Brown not just as a motivational speaker, but also as someone who can encourage anyone to be their own best friend and overcome obstacles when life feels hopeless. As it is in both recovery and life, hope heals, and this book will give you incredible hope. It's with great honor that I was able to write this foreword because it's true – *You've Got to Be HUNGRY!*

Best,

Joe Polish

# *Preface*

Immediately after writing *It's Not Over Until You Win*, originally published in 1997, I began preparing the manuscript for the book that you are now reading. I knew that I must write **You've Got To Be HUNGRY** so it's hard for me to believe that it has taken twenty-one years to complete this book! Not only does this book share the name of one of my most requested stories, but it also carries the essence of my most important message.

Those who listen to my messages know that I often speak about how so many people leave this earth without truly maximizing their potential, to live a  life of greatness. The people who take the time to cultivate and master their craft are the ones that we truly learn from. Perhaps what we admire most about these types of people is their ability to *become one with their gifts* and then *share those gifts* with the rest of the world.

I believe that we all have this ability to become one with our purpose and share it. We all have gifts and greatness within us given to us so that we can do something the world needs. My gift is delivering messages of hope and inspiration to others. My speeches, books, recordings, workshops, social media platforms, and every part of my public presence, are all crafted to inspire you to reach. I want you to reach your maximum potential and show up in the next level of your life in an impactful and powerful way.

Since the publishing of my first book, I have been fortunate enough to speak to billions of people around the world *(in person and through social media)* and I have seen so much change. I've lived through some amazingly beautiful experiences in my seventy-five years on earth. I have also had some very challenging, devastating, life-threatening experiences that would have taken the average person out. I want to share with you how I managed to still come out on top and win in those situations!

The application of the methods, principles, and the examples in this book will empower you to overcome every adverse circumstance, tragedy, setback, or challenge that life throws your way. I feel this book will introduce you to the life that you truly desire to live. I aim for this to be, not just another book you read, but a deep life-transforming experience!

Therefore, I encourage you to join our online

community *www.iamhungrylesbrown.com* to watch my coinciding teaching videos and complete the interactive e-learning courses. in the front of the book for more information.

I would love to connect with you. Please reach out to me on social media and introduce yourself! And remember: No matter what happens in life...

## You Have Greatness Within You!

# *You've Got to be HUNGRY*

# Table of Contents

# The Greatness Within to Win

## Introduction: Buried Treasure

Introduction

# Buried Treasure

You've GOT TO Be HUNGRY!

**"Blessed are those who HUNGER and thirst after righteousness for they shall be filled" (Matthew 5:6).**

*"It must be borne in mind that the tragedy of life doesn't lie in not reaching your goal. The tragedy lies in having no goal to reach. It isn't a calamity to die with dreams unfulfilled, but it is a calamity not to dream. It is not a disaster to be unable to capture your ideal, but it is a disaster to have no ideal to capture. It is not a disgrace not to reach the stars, but it is a disgrace to have no stars to reach for. Not failure, but low aim, is sin."*

*~Dr. Benjamin Mays~*

## *Don't Become Buried Treasure!*

Imagine this: You're on your deathbed and standing around your bed are the ghosts of the dreams and ideas given to you throughout life. Imagine that, for whatever reason, you never pursued those dreams. You never acted on those ideas. You never used those gifts. Imagine there they all are standing around your bed with large, angry eyes looking at you, saying, "We came to you and only you could have given us life and now we must die with you forever!" Dr. Howard Thurman

The question is:

*If you died today — what dreams, what ideas, what gifts, what inventions, what innovation, what voice, what story would die with you?*

As I mentioned in the Preface, I began writing this book in 1997. I didn't just walk away from writing this book twenty-one years ago though. I started and paused the work on this book several times throughout the years, as a lot of "life was happening" to me. As a matter of fact, my life was writing the pages of this book that entire period. However, one night while out eating dinner, I knew that it was finally time.

You see, upon tasting the food, I was instantly reminded of a meal that I'd eaten years ago that had been prepared by my best friend, Alexander Whyms (Bou). Cooking came naturally and easily to Bou. Even though Bou was very nonchalant about his gift of cooking, he refused to share any of his recipes with anyone. He guarded them like treasures (and they were) because he always said that "one day" he was going to write a cookbook. I encouraged him to do so, telling him that I would even write the Foreword, as a witness to his skills! Everything Bou cooked was uniquely delicious and amazing. We all begged him to share just some of the ingredients he used, but he would never tell any of us — *not even me!*

Eating that meal reminded me of being at Bou's funeral. As I was leaving the cemetery, a mutual friend approached me. She asked me if Bou had ever written his cookbook. Sadly, I had to tell her that he hadn't. I can so clearly remember her reaction. She responded with such deep disappointment, "OMG". He took that with him. He took all of that with him."

The never to be seen cookbook and all those incredible recipes died with Bou. Remembering that moment made me decide to refocus my energy on writing **You've Got To Be HUNGRY!** I know firsthand that tomorrow is not promised. As I tell my family often, "We can't get out of life alive." All of us have an expiration date and I decided that I was going to complete this book before mine arrived!

Dr. Myles Munroe, the great preacher, and orator said, "The wealthiest place on the planet is not in the Far East where there is oil in the ground. It's not South Africa where there are diamond mines. The wealthiest place on the planet is the cemetery. For there you will find leaders who have never stepped up; innovations the world has never been exposed to; talent and potential never realized.

I am reminded of another man who said, "Oh GOD! To reach the point of death only to realize you have never lived; only to realize that you never scraped the surface of your potential." I remember reading about a woman who had just left the doctor's office after having been told she had terminal cancer. She made herself a cup of coffee when she returned home. As she sipped it, she was suddenly filled with rage and hurled the cup against the wall, shattering it into pieces. As she threw it, she screamed out, "I REFUSE TO DIE AN UNLIVED LIFE!"

The truth is, everybody *dies*, but not everybody *lives*. People are born full of hope, wonder, and dreams, but then life happens, and those dreams are beaten out of them. I believe most people are unprepared for adversity and therefore, change directions. Instead of moving toward their dreams, they begin to move toward the grave long before they breathe their last breath. Maybe that is why one poet said, "Many a flower has bloomed and wasted its sweetness on the cold desert air."

Let me be totally honest with you, on the path to your dreams, there will be many interruptions. When you get on an airplane, the flight attendant announces that you must fasten your seatbelt in preparation for the inevitable turbulence. It is the same way with life. You must fasten your mental, emotional and spiritual seatbelts because you will experience turbulence. The only way that you can break through the atmosphere and reach higher altitudes is *by being HUNGRY!*

HUNGER is the most crucial element of creating your greatest life! For five decades, I've spoken passionately about this force called HUNGER. I have told many stories that illustrate how it has been the reason that I was able to overcome tragedies, failures and major illnesses — how it has been the catalyst for my many successes in life and has led to greatness. You too, have greatness in you — greatness that can only be recognized as you pursue your dreams — greatness that is unleashed and driven by the GOD-force in you that I call *HUNGER*.

HUNGRY people are seeking higher ground. People that are HUNGRY invest in themselves. HUNGRY people are willing to take the time to be still and shut the distractions of the world outside. HUNGRY people engage in deep reflections and ask themselves revealing questions. *"You must be* willing to *do the things today that others won't do, in order to have the things tomorrow that others won't have"* **Dr. Michael Kelley** People that are HUNGRY don't let life define them — they define themselves!

## *Hunger Personified*

**The chronicles of history reveal HUNGER personified in the lives of many great legends, as exampled following:**

Indian activist, **Mahatma Gandhi,** who was a leader and guru, had a HUNGER for peace and justice. One of his sayings was, "Live as if you were to die tomorrow. Learn as if you were to live forever." Amid great injustices, he refused to resort to violence to fight for equality. Without the use of weapons, he led his people to independence.

**Rosa Parks**, a woman living in Alabama in the 1950s, refused to move to the back of the bus and give up her seat to a white man. Even though she was seated, she stood up on the inside, as her HUNGER for justice gave rise to the Civil Rights movement.

Her actions caught the attention of **Dr. Martin Luther King, Jr.**, a young Baptist minister. He picked up the baton and became A Drum Major for Justice. His HUNGER to empower his people to live the American Dream, as opposed to the American Nightmare, resulted in the greatest advancement of human rights in the 20th century.

**Nelson Mandela** catalyzed change. His HUNGER to dismantle the shackles of apartheid helped him survive an undeserved twenty-seven-year prison sentence. Upon release, he quickly went from prison to the presidency and defeated, not only the South African government but also the United States government, who supported apartheid.

**Cesar Chavez**'s HUNGER for social and economic justice for migrant workers legitimized their struggle with nationwide support. He co-founded the National Farm Workers Association, which served as a powerful voice and platform for migrant workers, changing their lives forever.

# *You've Got to be HUNGRY*

Born in a storefront apartment, **Margaret Thatcher** had a HUNGER for politics at an early age. After losing her first two parliamentary elections, she paused to give birth to twins. Undaunted by losses and the responsibilities of motherhood, Thatcher went on to become the first female Prime Minister of Britain and the longest-serving British Prime Minister of all time.

With a HUNGER to care for the impoverished, disabled, and helpless of our society, **Mother Teresa** gave her life so that others could live theirs. She was awarded the Nobel Peace Prize in 1979 and canonized as Saint Teresa of Calcutta in 2016. Mother Teresa is recognized as one of the greatest humanitarians of the 20th century.

**Oprah Winfrey,** molested as a child and impregnated at fourteen, still rose to unprecedented heights, starring in the highest-rated talk show of its kind in history. Her HUNGER to succeed drove her to make a mark on the universe and leave an unforgettable legacy. She never allowed her past to dictate her future.

**Tyler Perry,** the world-renowned producer, playwright, entrepreneur, and philanthropist, rose above an abusive childhood and chronic depression. He went on to be named by Forbes as the highest-paid man in entertainment, earning $130 million in one year. His HUNGER to change Hollywood drove him to open a 330-acre movie studio compound in Atlanta, Georgia, even creating his own "Walk of Fame" for those who have been ignored.

**Barack Obama,** possessed with a HUNGER to make a difference, went from South-Side community activist to the White House. Even though he initially lost his first run for Senate, he was not deterred and eventually won. He then went on to win the most powerful title in the world — President of the United States. Not only was Barack Obama the first African American President of the U.S., but he is also, to date, the most admired President in United States history!

Beside every good man is a *great* woman, and **Michelle Obama** exemplified this truth — a woman whose story inspires us to HUNGER for and go after greatness! A graduate of Harvard Law School, Michelle gracefully established a legacy as the only African American to ever serve as First Lady of the United States.

Since her time in office, she has gone on to take the spotlight as one of the most coveted female motivational speakers in the world.

These mentioned legends are no different than you and I. The same HUNGER to live an impactful life that operated through them is available to us as well. Just like all of us, they had their challenges, failures, and setbacks. However, they got up and continued the journey, pressing toward the higher calling. As Marcus Garvey would say, "Rise up you mighty people, onward and upward to victory." You, have greatness in you that is lying dormant – HUNGER waiting to be called forth, waiting to inspire you to *live a life that will outlive you!*

## *Your Past is not Through with you Yet*

As you are working toward your goals and walking into your destiny, keep in mind that we cannot control time. I think twenty-one years is a pretty long time to be working on a book — *wouldn't you agree?* Everything may not come together right when you want it to. In fact, it may not come together for quite a while. We don't always know the time when our dreams will come to fruition. It's like asking when a baby will walk or talk — it happens when it happens. Over the years, as I worked with many wonderful people on this book, I always knew that something was missing. It kept haunting me, but I couldn't quite put my finger on it. Then suddenly one night as I slept with my TV on, I was awakened by the sound of the movie *Magnolia*. It was a line in the movie that called to the depths of my heart and awakened my soul. The words resonated with me so deeply that I could not go back to sleep after hearing them: *"We may be through with our past, but the past isn't through with us."*

I began to think about my own experiences and the experiences of others that I know. I wondered why immigrants can come to this country with barely any resources. Many of them lack formal education and have no understanding of our language — yet they are, statistically, three-to-four times more likely to achieve the American Dream than the average citizen born in America! That's when it hit me: ***There are things that we have experienced in the past that are impacting our present and compromising our future due to the damaging mental conditioning we've been subjected to.***

## *You've Got to be HUNGRY*

Studies indicate that by the time we are five years old, we have already determined what is, and is not, available to us. This is because, between the ages of zero and five, our brains soak up everything in our environment. This includes circumstances and situations, the conversations we hear, and the people around us. Those of us who have been exposed to toxic and mentally debilitating programming, programming that has been unrelentingly instilled in us over decades and reinforced on every level of life — can't just be told, "Be positive and enthusiastic; have a burning desire and you can live your dream!" Mere words won't do!

Some people are born into a culture where their sense of self has been destroyed — compromised by the government, religion, education, and racism — a culture where they are systematically marginalized. The odds of success are stacked against the average person and have been for centuries. Many people find the reach for success disheartening; they feel hopeless and powerless. I believe that is why the suicide rate is soaring. As Richard Wright so eloquently wrote, "The impulse to dream has been slowly beaten out of me by the experiences of life." To make it against all odds and snatch victory from the jaws of defeat, *You've Got to Be HUNGRY!*

I think that for most of us, our sense of self is so damaged that we must treat our minds like we would approach waxing a floor: **We must strip away the old before we apply the new.** Understanding this was the missing link that prevented me from completing this book sooner. I now realize that to help people whose vision of themselves has been severely compromised and in many cases destroyed, you must take their pre-existing mental condition into account. To help them achieve greatness, you must provide methods, tools and a process that will allow them to get out of their heads, out of their history, and into their imaginations.

The imagination is the only part of us that cannot be shackled. It is the irreducible essence of who we are, and it is that which allows us to see into our future. Einstein said, "The imagination is the preview of what is to come." Every chapter in this book, and the various tools created to coincide with it, have been designed to inspire you to preview and create the life that you were destined to live — Everything happens first in your mind and then in your reality. It is time for *your past to be through with you:* For you to step into the future of your imagination, step into the greatness that I will show you how to see!

To access that greatness, you must strip away your damaged sense of self and reprogram your mind; the hidden power catalysts of personal achievement revealed in this book will allow you to do just that. By going through this process, you will be able to tap into the truth of who you really are. You will access the freedom to operate from your greatness and live the life you were **chosen** to live.

I KNOW based upon my own experience that you are no accident. You were chosen out of hundreds of millions of sperm cells to do something great with your life! **You were created on purpose, for a purpose, and with a purpose!** You are a masterpiece because **you are a piece of The Master!** You have something special. You have greatness within you, but **You've Got to Be HUNGRY!**

# *The Greatness Within to Win*

## Chapter One: If I Was A Man NOW

# Chapter One

# If I Was A Man NOW

# HUNGER Defined

'␣ve been asked on numerous occasions — in interviews, at events, and even when people recognize me while walking in airports — to describe the one thing that has made me successful throughout my career as a radio host, television personality, politician, life coach, and speaker. I usually tell them that I had a goal to make my mother proud. Most people are satisfied with that answer, but occasionally, someone will probe a little deeper; some people want to know when my HUNGER was *triggered*.

If there was **ONE DEFINING MOMENT, in which I can say my HUNGER was born,** *the story I'm about to share with you next reveals that moment...*

## *If you're Hungry and you know it, Clap your Hands*

Growing up, my mother worked a variety of jobs to keep food on the table, clothes on our backs and a roof over our heads. Sometimes I had to go to work with

Mama because she couldn't find anyone to keep me — apparently, I was too much to handle *(smile!)* There was a day that Mama agreed to cover for our next-door neighbor, Ms. Ruby, who was ill at the time. Ms. Ruby worked for a wealthy family with the last name Harris. Mama would be serving the Harris's in place of Ms. Ruby while she recovered.

Although Mama didn't work for the Harris's regularly, she often worked for wealthy families on Miami Beach. She cleaned, cooked and cared for their children. We were allowed to eat the leftover food from the families that she served. I appreciated their generosity, but I wanted to be able to buy our own food. Mama watched over the children of the affluent and we wore their hand-me-down clothes. I was glad to have clothes to wear, but I wanted to be able to wear clothes that had never been worn before.

When we rode the bus to Miami Beach, we passed by signs that read, *"Jews, Dogs, and Coloreds Not Allowed."* There was a white line on the floor of the bus that divided the front from the back, where Coloreds had to stand. No matter how much room was available in the front, we had to stay behind that line. I can remember times when the back of the bus was so crowded that we Blacks were spilling over past the line, struggling to cram ourselves tighter together into the back of the bus. If I stepped one pinky-toe over that line, Mama would frantically snatch me back and scold me, "You have to stay behind the line, Leslie!"

We lived in the segregated South. Everything around us was designed to destroy our sense of self and our desire for a better life. But I still wanted a better life anyway. However, merely *wanting* something is not enough. It takes more than *want* to overcome odds that are stacked against you. It was on that day that I would experience a life-defining moment that would introduce me to what *"more than want"* really means.

As I rode past signs that announced I was unwelcomed in the country of my birth, on a bus that said I wasn't good enough to be in the front, a bus that charged me the same money to stand crowded in the back that it charged a White person to ride in a roomy seat in the front, infuriated me. Unbeknownst to me, the life-changing experience that I was about to have loomed ominously around me. And because the experience involved my mother, what was created in me that day, life would never be able to shake! That was the day that I gave birth to a *FIERCE HUNGER* that consumes me to this very moment!

It started once we arrived at Ms. Harris's home. I was assigned to rake leaves and then clean spots off the kitchen floor. While scrubbing away those spots, Ms. Harris sat at the table with her morning coffee. Barely raising her head from the newspaper that she was reading, she ordered my mother, "Mamie, go into the other room and find my purple and yellow hat! I want to wear it today."

My mother went into the room and soon afterward, I heard something — my mother was clapping her hands. I was curious, so I called out to her, "Mama!"

"What is it, boy?" said Mama.

"Why are you clapping your hands?"

"Don't you worry about it," she answered softly.

After a short while, she came out to report to Ms. Harris that the hat wasn't in the room she had checked. Ms. Harris sent her to check in another room and when my mother got in that room, she started clapping her hands again.

I called out, "Mama!"

"What is it, Leslie?" Mama was obviously annoyed, as my questions were distracting her from the task at hand.

"Why are you clapping your hands?" I demanded.

"I said don't worry about it. Just pay attention to what you're doing."

Ms. Harris then rudely stomped over to me. "I'll tell you why she's clapping her hands, boy!"

Looking up from the pail of water I was using and with the washcloth still in my hand, "Why, Ma'am?" I said.

Ms. Harris was glaring down at me very smugly. "She's looking for something for me. When I have Colored people looking for something where I can't see them, I make them clap their hands to make sure they're not stealing something in there."

I immediately dropped the washcloth and stood up with tears on my face and anger in my heart. I knew I was taking a chance because, at that time, we weren't supposed to look White people in the eyes, let alone speak back to them. Nonetheless, I spoke to her with defiance. "My mother, Ma'am, is not a thief. She's an honest woman. When she comes to replace Ms. Ruby, she won't steal from you and she won't steal from no one!"

Ms. Harris looked at me coldly and walked away without a single word.

I got back on my knees to resume my work. The water falling from my eyes joined the cleaning water in the pail. With a tear-soaked washcloth and a heart full of rage, I continued to scrub the floors.

That was the day — *that was the moment* — when my HUNGER was triggered. At that very moment, I made a commitment that my mother would never again have to work in a humiliating environment. Never again would she be in a situation where someone would make her clap her hands because they thought she might steal something. That experience changed my life... *I was never the same.*

## *Whatever it Takes*

As we sat on the bus heading back from Miami Beach toward home, I didn't talk much. That was unusual for me. I loved to talk and listen to Mama tell me stories. But that day, I just stared out the window. I was furious, as indicated by my countenance and the tears running down my cheeks. Not noticing my tear-stained face, Mama inquired,

"What's wrong, Leslie? You ain't said much." "I'm mad."

"Mad about what?"

I continued to look out the window and spoke sharply, full of venom, "Because I'm not a man! If I was a man right now, I could work and take care of you!"

In a reassuring and supportive manner, my mother attempted to comfort me. "You'll be a man soon enough. You're ten years old already."

I appreciated her encouragement, but *"soon"* was not good enough for me. "I wanna be a man NOW! If I was a man NOW, we would never have to wait for no leftover food! If I was a man NOW, we would never wear no clothes other people been wearing all year! If I was a man NOW, nobody wouldn't ever make you clap your hands for thinking you that you might steal something!"

She looked me in the eyes, with amazement and shock. "Ms. Harris told you that, didn't she?"

"Yes, Ma'am, and if I was a man RIGHT NOW, you would only cook for our family! You would cook for me. I would pay your bills and you would never go through that again!" I turned and glared out the window, looking at

45

the tourists relaxing on the beach, being entertained and enjoying life. "Mama, why can't we sit on Miami Beach like those people, and have carpet on the floor, and air conditioning, and have a big beautiful home, like Ms. Harris?"

"We just can't, Leslie!" Mama snapped back at me, as she looked away and fiddled with her dress.

"Why, Mama?" I was relentless. My HUNGER wanted answers!

Mama stopped fiddling with her dress and turned to me with a no-nonsense look. "Stop asking so many questions!" She made it clear my questions caused her to be uneasy, so I huffed and turned my attention back to looking out the window. My conversation with Mama was over, but the conversation within myself continued for a very long time.

I remember that day so clearly. As the bus drove into our neighborhood, there was contrasting poverty. Desperate, distraught, and destroyed-looking people were going about their daily routine — strolling on cracked sidewalks, littered with trash and despair. I observed that some of the people appeared satisfied with their surroundings, while others wore the stress of discontentment on their faces, while yet others were simply too intoxicated to care. *But for me?* I was HUNGRY to care for my mother. I was HUNGRY to take us out of that neighborhood. I was HUNGRY to live a larger life. *That HUNGER became my magnificent obsession.*

**Have you ever experienced something in your life that birthed a resolve in you to say, "No matter what it takes?"**

That's how I felt at that moment. No matter what it took, I knew that I would always be there to protect and provide for my mother. I was HUNGRY; failure was not an option! I knew that I had to make sure no one would ever humiliate her again. Very soon after that incident, I began to look for work to help support the family. I knew we were facing a lot of injustices during that time. However, that only stirred an even stronger determination to do what was in my heart.

I delivered newspapers, did yard work, cleaned houses, and did other odd jobs. I collected old pieces of metal and copper, old refrigerators, and fans and took them to Pepper's Junkyard for a few bucks. I also did day labor. Groups of us would stand around on a corner, hoping to be hired. Eventually, someone would arrive in a pickup truck and say, "Hey, boy, come here." Several of us would load into the truck and be taken to various places around town to move furniture and other heavy items. Today, whenever I see day laborers standing on a corner, hoping for work, I think to myself, *"That used to be me."*

Being subjected to this harsh lifestyle fueled me even more. I began to visualize how my family and I would feel living in a fancy mansion and not just cleaning one. I wanted Mama to laugh and enjoy life like the women I saw vacationing on the beach and those living lavish lives. I knew that we deserved to not only dream of this type of life but to LIVE it — *and I had a HUNGER to create it for us*. My HUNGER was unleashed the day I witnessed my mother being humiliated. As a matter of fact, I would say it was that day, in my heart, that I wrote the very first pages of *You've Got To Be HUNGRY!*

Later in life, I was blessed with a great Jewish mentor named Sam Axelrod. During his time mentoring me, Sam often spoke of the Jewish mantra, "Never Again". The mantra is a declaration of Jewish people's commitment to freedom and equality as a people. *Never Again* will they tolerate themselves being mistreated or exterminated like unwanted pests!

When I got older, I went to Poland to tour the Jewish concentration camps in Sam's honor. We had planned to go together but Sam died before we made it. While there, I laid eyes on over two tons of hair that was shaved from the heads of Jewish people during the Holocaust. I saw the gas chambers that were designed to look like showers. The Jews had been tricked into believing they'd be taking showers only to be gassed to death — their bodies then thrown in heaps into crematories and burned. I read the many names of the deceased on the commemorative walls. By the end of the tour, I finally understood what Sam had been teaching me those many years — *NEVER AGAIN!* I believe that we have all had some type of experience that causes us to cry out that infamous Jewish mantra, *Never Again*. Watching my dear Mama be humiliated and disrespected that day was my *Never Again* moment.

**Don't despise your *Never Again* moments, *for if you survive* them, no obstacle in your path will ever be able to hold you back or stop you!**

# You've Got to be HUNGRY

## *Understanding HUNGER*

The lion is, arguably, the most magnificent and majestic beast in the jungle and a most ferocious hunter. Motivated by HUNGER, the lion hunts down its prey with skill, precision, and determination. He is fearless and cunning. He doesn't give up. I'm convinced that humankind must operate from this same principle of HUNGER to fulfill dreams and to achieve greatness.

HUNGER is undeniably the most powerful force in the world, more dynamic than thirst or fear. HUNGER, in effect, conquers all other natural desires. This HUNGER is what fueled former British Prime Minister, Benjamin Disraeli, to say, "Nothing can resist a human will, that will stake even its existence on its stated purpose." The great military leader, Napoleon Bonaparte, alluded to this HUNGER in his statement, "An army marches on its stomach."

*The Book of Life* is forever a source of guidance that says, "Know ye not that you are the temple of GOD and the Spirit of GOD lives in you?"[1] There is a power and there is a presence in you that is waiting to be tapped into. This power is what allows you to manifest your greatness. I call this power HUNGER. Many gifted people, and average people alike, have used this power. These esteemed individuals have answered the call of HUNGER, the GOD-force circulating deep within.

In his classic book *Think and Grow Rich*, Napoleon Hill talks about the benefit of having a "burning desire." Having the desire to be successful is obviously a requirement for achieving that success. However, in today's world, I believe that it will take a little more. *How do you achieve the things that you desire in a world where the odds are stacked against the average person?* Some research suggests that only one percent of people will achieve the success they dream of!

If you want to be a part of that one percent, you must reach past *desire* and be HUNGRY to overcome the odds, disadvantages, setbacks, and tragedies that life will invariably throw at you! HUNGER is the precursor to amazing results — *incredible, unbelievable, inconceivable results!* HUNGER tramples "burning desire." HUNGER is but a distant cousin to mere *want*. Burning desire is just an infant when compared to the insatiable — refused to be denied — spirit that is driven by HUNGER! HUNGER is more than simple desire. HUNGER is a fortified and intensified expression of your higher self!

## *You've Got to be HUNGRY*

HUNGER is the foundation of your greatest life — on steroids! HUNGER is heart-centered and spiritually-fortified; it is a gut-based drive. HUNGER is the motivation behind all creation, innovation, and breakthroughs. I believe that all major accomplishments in life have happened by a person, or group of people possessed with a sense of HUNGER!

HUNGER is the driving force behind personal achievement! HUNGER is a multiplier, giving you more for less. HUNGER rewards your actions, producing results as if you are doing five times, ten times or maybe even one hundred times more than you are! HUNGER undeniably multiplies the efforts and effectiveness of the outcome! Without the drive and motivation of HUNGER, you will never have the compounded power that it grants you. YOU NEED HUNGER!

HUNGER is a GOD-force that exists deep down in the sanctuary of your soul. HUNGER is a magnificent obsession. HUNGER is released when you are in pursuit of your goals and dreams. HUNGER brings out your greatness. HUNGER, as Elizabeth Browning would say, *"releases the imprisoned splendor."* The truth is, to live the life you dream of, ***You've Got to Be HUNGRY!***

## <u>*Magic Leaves Don't Work*</u>

When I attended Booker T. Washington High School, one of my classmates was Larry Little, alumni of the Miami Dolphins. I recall seeing Larry, alone, running around the tracks in the burning-hot sun at Dixie Park. He had a vision of himself playing pro ball. Even though there were no coaches around telling him to do it or teammates to train with him, Larry was out there sweating, running and conditioning himself. I believe he was driven by HUNGER. The burning Miami sun did not matter; Larry kept on running toward his dream.

After college, Larry went on to play for the San Diego Chargers who later traded him to the Miami Dolphins for almost nothing, as if he had no value. Yet, Larry's dream of playing pro ball was realized — in a BIG way. Because of his HUNGER, he ended up being a part of the Miami Dolphins during one of their most winning seasons. He also became one of the few offensive guards, ever, to be inducted into the Football Hall of Fame!

*What did you dream about as a child? What HUNGER has been stirring in you for decades?*

## *You've Got to be HUNGRY*

Whether we realize it or not, we're all HUNGRY for something early in life. Growing up, I was HUNGRY for a better life. I loved watching and listening to the great orators of the day, who made that life seem possible: Dr. Martin Luther King, Jr., Dr. Norman Vincent Peale, Billy Graham and Malcolm X. I was mesmerized by the transformative impact they had on me and the audience. As a matter of fact, I am recalling a funny story about Brother Malcolm's "impact" on my life — or more accurately said, his "impact" on my behind. *(laugh)*

Malcolm X was a fire-filled speaker who always attracted a crowd. The first time I heard him, his words gave me an intense sense of pride and determination. After hearing Minister Malcolm speak, I was so fired up that I decided to change my name to Leslie X. When I got to school the next day and the teacher called my name for attendance, I didn't say, "Present," like I was supposed to. I didn't answer at all.

The teacher called my name again, with no response. She looked up from her desk and eyed me. "I knew I saw you. Yeah, there you are. Leslie Brown?"

I still didn't answer. The students around me began whispering, "Hey, she's calling your name."

I sat there at my desk, unbothered, and made a firm declaration, "That's not my name."

"Yes, it is! Yes, it is!" said the students.

"No, it's NOT." I refused to be deterred, as I continued to sit there, with my arms folded.

The teacher got up from her desk and walked over to me menacingly. She looked down at me intently, as I sat at my desk. "Leslie Brown?" Standing there with her hands on her hips and tapping her right foot impatiently, she waited for me to answer.

"My name is Leslie X!" I shouted.

"Is that right? Does your mother know about this?"

I told her I didn't know, at which point she informed me that she would be calling my mother immediately. She did just that, telling my mama that I had changed my name to Leslie X. When Mama heard the news, she said to the teacher, "send him home right away, so I can whip his behind until the cows came home!"

I wasn't worried about getting a beating that day though because I had a special anti-whipping good luck charm with me. You see, a few days before the Malcolm X event, an older gentleman in the park had given me some "magic leaves." They supposedly possessed the power to ward off all whippings! In my youthful naivety, I believed they would work, so I approached my mother with confidence when I returned home that afternoon.

Unfortunately for me, there was no magic in those leaves! Before I even had time to consider a change of heart, Mama had me upside down by the legs. The "magic leaves" started flying out of my pockets, as I screamed for mercy. Mama beat me all over the house **and** made me clean up those leaves too. *(laugh!)*

I'm here to tell you that the old saying — Don't let your mouth write a check that your butt can't cash — holds true! Mamie Brown didn't play that! Before the night ended, I came to my senses and reclaimed my given name of Leslie Brown. The next morning at school, when the teacher called out my name, you can bet your bottom dollar I said with a very strong and clear voice, **"PRESENT!"**

## *What Are You Hungry For?*

Although my mother would not permit me to change my last name to 'X', it's important to note the impact that Dr. Martin Luther King, Jr. and Brother Malcolm X had on me. They made me want to take action and made me willing to take risks! I was drawn to something in them. Their words and their delivery resonated deep in my heart. Even though at the time I didn't know it, I was preparing for my destiny. As I listened to and studied the great orators of my day, my HUNGER was leading me down my destined path.

Back in those days, I just seemed like a mouthy little kid. I was always being punished for talking too much. Now I get paid to speak all over the world! When I look back over my life, I realize I was born to inspire, motivate, and transform people's lives with my voice and my stories. I've been told by my children that I talk in my sleep. That doesn't surprise me. Speaking is what I do; it's who I am.

### *Who are you? What does the next greatest version of you look like?*

You must *KNOW* what you're HUNGRY for if you ever expect to have your dream. I remember the point in my life when I decided I was going to become a motivational speaker. My friends found it funny when I told them. They laughed at me and began to list all the reasons that it wouldn't work: "You don't have a college education; you don't have the money; you've never worked for a major corporation, and besides that, you have the complexion of rejection! It will never happen!" They reminded me of all the things I had worked against me and declared that with over 3,000 members of the National Speakers Association, I would never be able to attract an interested audience.

***My mother taught me something a long time ago:***
***"Opinions are like behinds, everybody's got one!"***
***Don't listen to your doubters. Listen to your***
***HUNGER!***

You must KNOW what you're HUNGRY for! You must know who you are! Not your legal name — that's just a label. It didn't matter if I was *Les Brown* or *Leslie X*. As a matter of fact, it didn't matter if I was called *Boy, Colored Boy* or *Mr. Nobody*. The only thing that mattered is that I would one day come to understand why I was born. Your reason and purpose for being born defines who you really are! *What are you HUNGRY for? Who are you called to be? What is your purpose? HUNGRY people know the answers to these questions.*

*"What lies behind us and what lies before us, are small matters compared to what lies within us. And when we bring what is within us out into the world, miracles happen."*

~ *Ralph Waldo Emerson*~

**Chapter 2: Two Women. One Purpose**

# Chapter Two

# Two Women, One

# Purpose

## HEART-Centered

## *Life, Love & Legacy*

As I'm gathering my thoughts to continue to share in this book, I'm reminded that my ability to do so is because of two women — the one who gave me life and the one who gave me love. My life began in a poor section of Miami, Florida, called Liberty City. I was born in an abandoned building, on a hard linoleum floor, along with my twin brother, Wesley. The woman who gave birth to us was not able to keep us. She agreed to give us to a lady named Ms. Mamie Brown, who we would come to know as Mama.

Wesley and I didn't know we were adopted until the age of seventeen. I never questioned my mama's love. But of course, I had questions about our origins. Fortunately, our godfather was there to convey the story of how Wes and I came into the life of Mamie Brown. This is how Mr. Moss told it...

Mamie Brown was unable to have children of her own. Over the years, she shared her desire with everyone, including her friend Mr. Moss, to have a child. After some time had passed, he heard of a young lady who had given birth to twin boys that she wanted to give up for adoption. The young lady's husband was away in the military when she got pregnant and gave birth to the twins. She was very fearful of how her husband would react and was desperately trying to find someone who would take both boys before her husband returned home.

Our birth mother had met several people who only wanted one of her twins, but she couldn't bear the thought of her boys not growing up together. When Mr. Moss found out about the situation, knowing that Mama wanted a baby, he asked her if she would be willing to take us both. Mama told him that she would love to have twin boys. Mr. Moss explained to her that time was of the essence, so Mama got dressed immediately and they left at once. They then drove to Liberty City to meet with our mother.

Our mother was waiting for them in the backroom of an abandoned building. When Mama and Mr. Moss arrived, Wes and I were wrapped in light blue blankets and she was holding us, one in each arm. Her eyes were red as if she had been crying. She seemed tired and drained when she asked Mama, "Are you the one who is going to take both my boys?"

Mama walked over to her and peered down at us. "Yes, I am."

Our birth mother came closer to Mama and when they were almost nose-to-nose, she looked her in the eyes intensely and said, "Do you promise to take good care of them and **never** to separate them?"

"Yes, honey. I promise to keep them together."

Our mother stood, looking Mama dead in her eyes for a few more moments. Finally, she broke the silence. "I believe in my heart you're the one who will take good care of my boys and keep them together. You're the one." She then handed us to Mama, leaned forward and kissed us both on the forehead and pleaded with Mama to go.

Mamie Brown took us both in her arms and began to walk to the car. Mr. Moss and our birth mother both walked closely behind Mama to help her get situated. Mr. Moss then got in the car and slowly started driving away. As he was driving, he and Mama heard a heart-wrenching scream. They turned around to see our mother running toward the car crying out.

"Wait! Wait! WAIT!"

Mama asked Mr. Moss if he thought our mother had changed her mind. He stopped the car and waited.

When our birth mother arrived at the car, she begged Mama again. "Please take care of my boys and don't separate them!"

As Mama held us tightly in her arms, she looked at our mother with eyes full of compassion and sincerity. "I promise you. I will not separate these boys and I will guard them with my very life."

The woman who gave us life then opened the car door. Wes and I looked up at her with wide eyes, as she kissed us one last time. "Mr. Moss, you can go now. Please go now." Mr. Moss drove off and that would be the last time that Wes and I ever laid eyes on our birth mother.

## Mamie Brown was HUNGRY

After entering the earth through the womb of my biological mother, GOD placed me in the heart of my adoptive mother. As I reflect on this, I feel like Abraham Lincoln who said, "All that I have and all that I hope to be, I owe to my mother." I love my mother very much and, just as important, I admire her. I admire her single-handed parenting, her courage, her faith and her determination. I have no shame admitting — **I am a Mama's boy**!

Although Mama never had any children of her own, she was HUNGRY to fill her life with children. My twin brother and I were among seven children that she took in as foster kids and later adopted. That should tell you a lot about who Mamie Brown was as a person. I would have to say that my HUNGER and drive for greatness was conceived through the upbringing of this great woman. She exemplified what I mean when I say *You've Got to Be HUNGRY!*

# HUNGRY stands for:

**H**eart-Centered

**U**nshakable Faith

**N**OW Urgency

**G**row Continuously

**R**elationship Impact

**Y**ES LORD

**Heart-Centered** — Every dream must be a HEART-CENTERED obsession that you are driven to achieve or acquire. You *believe* in your mind, but you *know* in your heart. HUNGRY people operate from their hearts!

**Unshakable Faith** — Going after your dreams requires you to have UNSHAKABLE FAITH. It doesn't really matter what happens *to* you; it matters what happens *in* you. HUNGRY people live faith-inspired lives!

**NOW Urgency** — You can't get out of life alive, so "live each day as if it's your last because one day it will be." HUNGRY people live with a sense of NOW URGENCY!

**Grow Continuously** — You don't get out of life what you want, you get out of life what you are. To have something you've never had before, you must become something you've never been before. HUNGRY people GROW CONTINUOUSLY to become what they need to be!

**Relationship Impact** — Relationships fall into one of two categories: nourishing relationships that bring out the best in you or toxic relationships that drain out the best of you. HUNGRY people are always asking themselves, "Who can I count on and who should I count out?"

**YES LORD** — HUNGER speaks to a calling deep within. You have greatness that is waiting for permission to show itself. HUNGRY people understand that their greatness is unleashed by saying *YES LORD!*

Mamie Brown had a **Heart-Centered** drive to have children. She had an **Unshakable Faith** that raising children was her destiny. She operated with a sense of **Now Urgency** to take possession of her dream. She did not take time to "think about it" or put it off until later; she went after it IMMEDIATELY! She knew how to **Grow Continuously**, as she personally developed the fortitude and knowledge to become both mother and father to her children. She understood the relevance of **Relationship Impact**, knowing who she could count on to help her with her dream. And when asked, "Do you promise to take good care of them and never separate them?" Mamie Brown simply said *'YES'* to her calling.

## *What's Your Dream*?

I believe that each one of us has a special calling on our lives, a work that we are assigned to do. For us to fulfill that which we are assigned to do, we must first be open to the truth that *it is possible*. As long as your heart is open to the possibilities, you will find that whatever you're seeking is also seeking you!

My birth mom was under a great deal of pressure to find a home for her twin boys, as quickly as possible. Yet, she turned down various people who attempted to separate me and my twin brother. Her dream was to give her children to *the right person*, one who would keep us together. She believed if she searched hard enough, she would find that person. My adoptive mother let everyone know that, although she could not have children of her own, she wanted a child to share her life with. She believed if she told enough people, she would find a child to call her own.

These two women each had a dream. One had a dream to find the right person to raise the children she'd given birth to and the other had a dream to raise children that she was unable to give birth to. Their HUNGER led them to each other to fulfill the calling of their hearts. Their *Heart-Centered* desire had become a magnificent obsession and thus was destined to manifest!

# *You've Got to be HUNGRY*

*What do you think about all the time? What do you talk about? If you could live life all over again, what would you do? What would you accomplish? What would your life look like?*

*The Book of Life* says, "I will give you the desires of your heart."[2] When it is a **Heart-Centered** obsession, I believe you can have it! I believe that every dream a person holds has been given to them by GOD. It is a HUNGER that He places in each of us so that we will aspire to greatness and live a life that will outlive us! I believe that life is GOD's gift to us and how we live our lives is our gift to GOD.

*I may not know you personally, but based upon my experience, here's what I know about you: You have something special! You have greatness in you! You can do more than you have ever imagined!*

However, I've come to know that most people go to their graves never discovering *why* they were born. Mark Twain stated, "The two most important days in your life are the day you were born, and the day you realize why you were born."

***Why were you born? What do you want out of life? You will not be able to live your life over again, so do as much as you can with the life you have left!***

Often when I travel, I ask people what they do for a living. The vast majority will tell me the kind of work they do. Then I will ask them if it's their passion. Most people will say that it's not. I follow up with the question, "Well, why do you do it then?" They answer that it pays the bills. I then gently urge them to search their hearts and ask them, "What are you living to do?" Nine out of ten of them will tell me about their dream life.

It's crucial, as you look at your life and into your future, that you follow your heart. When you do what's in your heart, you love it so much that you'll do it for nothing until you achieve a level of mastery. You'll eventually do it so well that people will pay you to do it! That's why the Book of Life says, "Where your heart is, there your treasure is also."[3] I strongly believe that no one was born to work for a living! Instead, you should aim to live your making because living your making will make your living!

**People who are HUNGRY go for their dream, against all odds. They believe as Dexter Yager who said, "If the dream is big enough, the odds don't matter!"**

## *Live A Heart-Centered Life*

Having the ability to live a **Heart-Centered** life consumes your total being. The heart is the dwelling place of the GOD- force that I call HUNGER. Gary Cox said, "If you are ever in an internal war between your mind and your heart, follow your heart." As a society, we've been educated to be logical, practical and realistic when considering pursuing our dreams. The truth is there are things you are capable of that your current logic is unable to process.

Logic has limitations. To believe something, the mind requires proof. The mind says, "I see it, so I believe it." The heart's response is, **"I know it, and that's why I see it!"** The mind *believes*, but the heart *knows.* The heart is connected to a presence and power in you that can preview your future. The heart taps into a knowing that flows from the center of your soul — a knowing that is not limited to what is practical and probable because the heart knows that all things are possible! *Live a Heart-Centered life!*

You will face hardships, setbacks and disappointments as you reach for your greatness. When you get knocked down in life, your mind will tell you to stay down. Your mind will tell you that there is just no way you can win. However, the heart will say that it doesn't matter how many times you get knocked down; it's how many times you get up! There are things that you know in your heart you can do, even though you've never done them before or even when you've failed at trying them in the past. Be inspired by your heart's *knowing* and do what it leads you to do!

I know of a man named Roland Tate who was given six months to live after being diagnosed with pancreatic cancer. Ninety-seven percent of individuals diagnosed with this cancer live only six to nine months and the other three percent have a life expectancy of only five years. Fortunately for Roland, he found a doctor who gave him a clock with no hands on it. After handing him the clock, the doctor said, "This is how much time you have to live." What the doctor meant was that it was up to Roland to determine the quality and duration of the life he lived!

Roland knew in his heart that he could beat pancreatic cancer even though the odds were against him. The odds are stacked against the average person, but when you live a **Heart-Centered** life, you rise far above average and all the odds are suddenly in your favor! Roland had a HUNGER to be here for his family.

He had a higher sense of purpose that was calling him, and he knew it was not his time to die. Roland consciously tapped into the HUNGER within to conquer his *so-called fatal* illness. Roland's HUNGER to live ignited a magnificent obsession to beat the odds and it has now been over eight years since his diagnosis!

Even when a doctor, with a stethoscope around his neck, says, "You're going to die"— it is the heart that will say, "You may determine the diagnosis, but GOD determines the prognosis!" No matter what you are facing or what you may face in the future, you can make it when you live a **Heart-Centered** life! The heart is not affected by the odds.

If it's merely *possible*, the heart says, *"Let's do this!"*

The heart does not *deny* the facts, but it *defies* the facts. Your heart is your superpower! When you've been flattened by life, it's your heart that will say, "It's not over until I win!"

**What's in your heart? Know what's in your heart and go after it. Let it become your magnificent obsession!**

## Don't Be Afraid to Walk Away

There is a Scripture in *The Book of Life*, which says, "Lean not to thine own understanding."[4] There is nothing wrong with searching for answers. However, we must always bear in mind how limited our understanding truly is. While we grapple with the *how* and *why* of life, destiny has things in store for us that are inconceivable to our limited understanding!

When I started my career as an Ohio state legislator, I was initially blown away at how far I'd ventured away from my dream of being a disc jockey. But I knew that my voice had power and that I could make an impact as a politician. I quickly found my footing as a politician and became active on several committees, including being appointed chair of the Human Resources and Education Committees.

# You've Got to be HUNGRY

I loved my work and felt that this could be my purpose in life. My mind was made up that politics was a solid career choice for me. After being re-elected to a third term, I decided that the next step for me was to run for State Senate and I began strategizing toward that end. I could have easily sung the popular song by McFadden and Whitehead, *Ain't No Stopping Us Now!* But then...

### ...life happened and one phone call changed everything.

One day as I was preparing for another successful day of politicking, I received a phone call from my sister, Margaret Ann. Despite the distance, my family and I made a point to stay in communication. I was excited to share the news of my latest plans with her. That changed immediately when I heard her voice.

Margaret Ann spoke in a very unsettling tone and I could tell that something was off. "Leslie, are you sitting down?"

Without another word, I responded instinctively. "What's wrong with Mama?" Everything in me already knew what that call was regarding! Her voice trembled. "Mama has breast cancer." Without missing a beat, I informed my sister that I was on my way. There are times that a single phrase can literally alter the course of your entire life. That was one of those times for me. Despite my success as a political power player, I knew without a shadow of a doubt that I needed to move back to Miami to help take care of Mama. Within an hour of the phone call, I made the decision to resign from office and bought a one-way plane ticket home.

Against the advice of many of my closest friends and mentors, I left everything behind — my home, furniture, car, clothes, and my political career. I returned to Miami the very next day, jobless. I had no clue *how* I was going to generate money to pay for the expensive traditional and alternative medical assistance that would be required for Mama's treatment. I wasn't nervous though because I had a feeling in my heart that things would work out for all of us. I chose not to worry about the *how*.

Even though I knew the split-second decision to pick up and leave everything behind would be best for my mother's well-being, I was taking a huge risk. Nonetheless, I had committed to be there for my mother when she needed me and that was my top priority. Sometimes you must walk away from everything that you've worked hard for, to answer the call of your heart!

## *You've Got to be HUNGRY*

Ultimately, it was the decision to walk away from the life I had built for myself that introduced me to a part of Les Brown that I'd never known

## *Follow Your Heart to GREATNESS*

*People say, "It's not over 'til the fat lady sings", but many people quit while she's just clearing her throat! Don't quit! Bet on you! When life introduces interruptions when challenges block your path, bet on you!*

Things were not easy when I first settled in Miami, but I was committed to my commitment and had no doubt that my HUNGER would lead me to a solution. I began to attend various seminars targeting entrepreneurship. One evening, I went to an event that hosted multiple speakers — Zig Ziglar, Jim Rohn, Dr. Norman Vincent Peale, and many others. Initially, I was there to take in the information, but after I took my seat and the speakers came on stage, something inside of me clicked.

It was like someone turned on a light switch inside of me. The energy of all the tapes I'd listened to, the men that I admired growing up, my experience in radio, my friends and family being engaged in my stories — it all began to come to me in waves and I said to myself, "Whoa, I can do this!"

During this epiphany another speaker stepped on stage As I was listening to him... I was imagining what I would say, if I were the one up there holding the microphone.  As if he could read my mind, he randomly shouted out, "Someone out there should be up here!"

I felt like I was having an out-of-body experience. I needed to tell someone! I jumped up, ran out of the room and found the closest payphone. I used ten cents to call my friend, Mike Williams. When he answered the phone, I screamed at him, "Mike, I'm not rejecting myself anymore!" Hearing the urgency in my voice, he told me to calm down, but I said again, "No, no, no! I'm not rejecting myself anymore! I figured it out— I'm gonna speak! This is how I'm gonna take care of my mother!" From that day forward, Mike Williams became my mentor and strategist.

After I hung up the phone, I went back inside and looked at the people on stage and thought, "I've finally figured it out. I know in my heart that I can do this!"

When the event was over, I went to my car. As other people were driving away, I sat there and reflected on all the jobs I'd worked where managers made my life a living hell. Those jobs never resonated with my heart because I was born to speak and change lives.

***Is there a major goal that you would like to achieve? Is there something that excites you that you feel is a calling?***

Believe me, it's best if the goal is beyond your comfort zone because to do something you've never done, you must become someone you've never been! It is natural to doubt yourself. As quickly as you can determine your goal, within seconds your own inner mind can cause you to doubt it. But I'm here to tell you that you don't know enough about yourself to be so cynical!

I have seen miracles occur in my life and in the lives of so many others who once doubted themselves and their potential. Miracles happened because we chose to follow our hearts to greatness. What's the over-riding voice in your head — the internal power voice — that governs your life and your vision of yourself? *The Book of Life* says, "Choose you this day, whom you will serve."[5]

*Which voice are you going to listen to? Will it be the voice of your heart or that small victim voice? Choose your heart, choose your superpower! Follow your heart to greatness!*

## Your Dream IS POSSIBLE!

At the opening celebration of one of the Disney theme parks, the staff members were talking amongst themselves. One of them remarked on how great it would have been if Walt had been there to witness all its wonder. Another employee replied, "Because he knew it would be, that's why we're here." In other words, Walt already *saw* it that's why we *see* it!

*Are you living the life that you have chosen or the life that's expected of you? What do you desire to do deeply?*

Like Walt, you must have a blueprint of your vision. There is a larger life waiting for you. There's a calling, a mission, an assignment waiting for you to accept it. This is not the time to be modest. We all have gifts and your dreams are waiting to be discovered. It's very important that no matter how long it takes, no matter the setbacks, no matter the challenges — *you KNOW that your dream is possible!*

## *You've Got to be HUNGRY*

For a long time, I did not think that my ability to communicate had any value. I mean after all; I was the kid who was labeled "educable mentally retarded" and left-back two grades! I was the kid who always got punished for talking too much! As far as I was concerned, I was *just talking*. I had no idea that once I stopped *just talking* and started speaking with purpose, I would change the lives of myself, my family, and millions of people worldwide!

Even after I decided that I wanted to be a speaker, I was still trapped in fear because my past was not through with me. I had convinced myself that the things I wanted and the life I saw in my future were unavailable to me. I was intimidated by what I thought I lacked — the credentials that other people had, the necessary resources, and the support I believed I needed. I knew I could have more, but I struggled with believing that I was good enough.

I truly believe, with all my heart, that we've been made in the likeness and image of GOD. I believe that we have been given authority and dominion over everything in our lives. But we will never walk in the power we've been given until we confront who and what we have not yet become. It was Dr. Carter G. Woodson who said:

*"If you can determine what a man shall think, you will never have to concern yourself with what he will do. If you can make a man feel inferior, you will never have to compel him to seek an inferior status, for he will seek it himself. If you can make a man feel justly an outcast, you will never have to order him to the back door. He will go there himself, and if there is no back door, his very nature will demand one!"*

We must reprogram our minds. *The Book of Life* says, "As a man thinketh, so is he, and as he continues to think, so he remains."[6] Earl Nightingale asked the question: "What's wrong with men today?" He answered the question by saying, "Men simply don't think!" Not only do we often not think, but even when we do think, we think with the wrong mind. This is why we must *re-think* our lives!

> **Many of You have been told a lie about yourself —**
> **that you're lacking and inadequate — don't believe**
> **it! You have everything you need to become all that**
> **you were born to be! Believe me!**

I once received a rejection letter from an infomercial company — the company that now promotes Tony

Robbins. The letter read: "We like your content, but we don't believe that the world is ready for a Black speaker." I normally didn't reply to rejections, but in this case, I made a special exception. I wrote back: "Thank you very much for letting me know that I'm Black. I never would have known it if you had not told me! I don't believe your company is progressive enough to receive my level of content. I'll see you from the top!" *Without their letter, I could still be confused about my identity to this day. (laugh)*

Helen Keller once said, "When one door closes, another one opens." But most people spend so much time complaining about the closed door, they don't realize that they can create another door for themselves — a door that will lead to untold opportunities that are waiting to be discovered. When you are in pursuit of your dreams, many doors will be closed in your face and some will not open at all. HUNGRY people will find a window or cut a hole in the roof or knock on the back door or sit in the parking lot, blowing their horn until somebody comes!

I was determined to overcome the rejection of the infomercial company, so I created another door for

84

myself! I made a proposal to the Public Broadcasting System (PBS) and they accepted. I produced six PBS specials, which they used during their fundraising periods. My PBS specials catapulted my career, increasing my exposure and dramatically improving my credibility. I even won a Chicago-area Emmy Award for my work on PBS. I went on to receive the much-coveted National Speakers Association Council of Peers Award of Excellence (CPAE), and ultimately, its most prestigious Golden Gavel Award for achievement and leadership in communication.

I was selected by Toastmasters International as one of the top five speakers in the world and I did it all despite being rejected for an infomercial!

Yes *me*, the one who was labeled educable mentally retarded. Yes *me*, the one whose friends laughed at him. Yes *me*, the one who had no resources or connections. Yes *me*, that poor boy from Liberty City, born on the floor of an abandoned building and given up for adoption. Yes *me*, Ms. Mamie Brown's Baby Boy! I'm thankful for those appearing obstacles they fueled my HUNGER!

# You've Got to be HUNGRY

*Don't you ever let any negative opinion —*

*whether it's yours or somebody else's —*

*determine who you are, what you can accomplish*

*or what your value is. **KNOW your dream is***

***possible. Listen to your heart!***

**Chapter 3: Excuse Me, Les Brown is Dying**

# Chapter Three

# "Excuse me, Les Brown Is Dying."

## Unshakable Faith

# The Greatness Within to Win

## From Heart-Centered to Unshakeable!

When I truly began to operate strictly from my faith, rather than my fear, new worlds opened to me. I encountered amazing experiences and saw the laws of attraction at work firsthand. It seemed like nothing was out of my reach, including the legendary and iconic soul singer, Gladys Knight, who I eventually had the honor of marrying.

One day, as she and I were riding around New York listening to the radio station, WBLS, I was feeling quite confident and empowered. I said to her, "You know, I used to be a DJ back in Miami and Ohio. I bet you I could convince them to put me on this station and I'll become a dominant force in this market."

Gladys was surprised and said, "No way!"

"You don't believe me? No problem. Let's go to the station now and watch what happens."

When we got to the station, as usual, everyone knew her and all but ignored my presence. I asked to see the general manager and someone went to get him. As we waited for him to arrive, everyone clamored around

Gladys asking for her autograph, still ignoring me!

The general manager came down to meet us and was excited to see Gladys. He then asked who I was.

I introduced myself to him in an attention-grabbing manner. "Hello, I'm Les Brown. Would you like to be the leading radio station in New York like you used to be?"

He looked at me like it was a dumb question. "Yes," he said, as he rolled his eyes.

"Great! Then hire me as your morning personality. I have the ability to do that for you." As I spoke, the conviction in my words, and my **Unshakeable Faith** in my ability to do exactly what I said I could, resonated with him. I know it was the look in my eyes that told him the only reason he was spared from birth control was to grant me this rare opportunity. *(laugh)*

Gladys watched closely as he and I talked for a few more moments. I told him that it would cost seven figures to make the deal. We stood looking at each other in silence. However, not long afterward and much to Gladys's amazement, he agreed to my price.

He gave us a date to come back and meet with their lawyers to sign the contract. On the day when I returned, the lawyers were present. One of them asked him if he had ever heard me on the radio. He timidly answered, "No." I guess that must've shaken him a bit. He looked over at me and asked, "Can you really make this show a success?"

I smiled at them all. "Absolutely, I can, and I will!" We then signed the contract!

If you want to create something in life, you must operate with a sense of *knowing*, as I did on that day. Whatever your goals are — personally, professionally or some cause that you believe in — you must have **Unshakeable Faith** in your ability to do it. That day, I went from being thought of as one of the Pips to the Conductor of the Midnight Train!

Even though I had not been on the radio in years, I knew I could do it. My attitude was: Give me a microphone and the airwaves and I can turn any city upside down! My first morning on-air, the general manager called in after ninety minutes of listening to me and said, "Wow! You can really do this, can't you?" My faith in my ability showed up in the ratings. The Platinum Playing Papa was back on the air...with a bang!

# You've Got to be HUNGRY

## _Joy and Pain..._

I was finally back on top after walking away from everything to take care of Mama. Life was going great for me. I was pursuing my dream to be a full-time speaker, I was married to the beautiful Gladys Knight, and I was back on the air in New York. I could not have been happier!

One of my favorite songs is _Joy and Pain,_ by Frankie Beverly and Maze. I think the lyrics offer a perfect explanation of the duplicity of life. Just as there are highs in life, there will surely be lows. Certainly, it would be great if every day were perfect with no hiccups. But the truth is, life can be messy. Things can be going great for a long while with everything moving in the right direction. Then, suddenly, with no warning — life will slap you down!

**You will be tested on what you believe. Are you ready to PROVE that your faith cannot be shaken?**

I was about to be tested, BIG TIME! But in the meantime, I was going along my happy way doing what I loved. I always aim to use my platforms to serve the community as much as possible. Therefore, when I became aware that the rates of prostate cancer were on the rise and that there was a huge push for testing, I started a campaign to encourage men to get prostate exams.

As part of the campaign, I invited a doctor on my show to share his expertise on the issue. On the day of his interview, he asked me the (not so) obvious question, "Have *you* been tested?" That question had never crossed my mind until then. I suppose I just thought I was the picture of perfect health. Although I was leading the charge for other men to get tested, it never occurred to me that I, too, needed to take the test for myself!

After learning that I had not been tested, the doctor convinced me to come into his office to get a test done. A few days afterward, he called me to schedule a consultation. I could hear in his voice that the news wasn't good. I didn't want to wait so I told him to tell me over the phone. He then said the four words that no man ever wants to hear: "You have prostate cancer."

I was floored! There I was rallying the cause to save other people's lives when it was my life that needed to be saved! A wise man once said, "Coincidence is GOD's way of staying anonymous." Even though I was just trying to impress Gladys when I walked into WBLS, I now realize that was a GOD moment. I had no symptoms when I was diagnosed with cancer. Had it not been for me landing that position, I most likely wouldn't have discovered the cancer until it was too late!

*Things are going to happen to you in life that you can't anticipate. You will have setbacks and disappointments. The storms of life will come.*

It's easy to have faith when everything is working right — bills are paid, kids acting like they have good sense, your relationship is working, etc. But when challenged with overwhelming and seemingly insurmountable obstacles,

*Unshakeable Faith* is required! Somehow, for many people, it is during these challenges that faith sneaks out the back door, running quickly. Fear comes in the front door, demands a cup of coffee, takes a seat and says, "Give me a newspaper. I'm gonna be here for a while."

# The Greatness Within to Win

*Greatness requires Unshakable Faith. It doesn't matter what happens to you; it matters what happens in you... and most importantly how you handle it!*

I remember talking to the doctor, Alfred Goldstein, the day he told me that I had prostate cancer. Dr. Goldstein has a great sense of humor. When I asked him if he could get me a second opinion, he looked at me intently and said, "Yes, and you're ugly too."

We both laughed so hard! A brother couldn't get a break that day! But the laughter was so needed. Dr. Goldstein helped to dispel the fear of the word *cancer* — the most feared word in seven different languages. We both knew the road ahead would be tough. He needed to help me to set the stage for how I was going to handle my crisis. It was up to me if I was going to allow what was happening *to* me to dictate what was happening *in* me.

*"When the going gets tough, the tough get going!"*

*Billy Ocean*

## *A Boxing Match with Murphy*

Once I realized what I was facing, I had to remove all the things that might hinder my healing process. I needed to focus on my health. This meant quitting my job in radio. Being at that status in radio was a career-high for me. I enjoyed living in New York and I really felt that I had begun to impact the city. It was so challenging for me to have to tell the general manager about my decision to leave. However, he told me that he understood. He seemed to have compassion for me and said that he would be praying for my recovery.

When I got home after our meeting, my phone was ringing off the hook. Each time I answered, a crying friend or relative was telling me how sorry they were to hear the news and asking was there anything they could do to help. I had no clue what was going on until a friend told me what had taken place. The station manager had gone on the air with a public service announcement: "Les Brown is dying. He's been diagnosed with prostate cancer." He ended his announcement with: "Good luck, my brother. We'll be praying for ya!"

I knew this man didn't like me, but I didn't think he would do something like that! There are levels to anger and I was at the level of Incredible Hulk — I saw green, red, black, and a ton of other colors and stars! I wanted to run down to the station and grab him by the neck. I am reminded of a verse in a song that says, "You gonna make me lose my mind, up in here, up in here. You gonna make me act a fool, up in here, up in here!" *(laugh)*

Not only did he share my private and confidential information on the air, but he also publicly humiliated me by putting me in a casket before I was dead! The fight for my life was much more important than confronting him. For me to win it, I needed all the strength that I had.

Something welled up inside me that said, "This is not going to take your life!" I knew that GOD wasn't through with me yet. I decided that I wasn't going to die for a very long time and that I was going to become a cancer conqueror! At the time, my PSA — which stands prostate-specific antigen — was as high as 2,400. The normal range is between 2.5 and 4.0. I decided to make PSA stand for Positively Staying Alive!

I had **Unshakeable Faith** and I was determined to use it! However, despite my faith, the battle for my life, my destiny, and my purpose was intense!

*Is your faith strong enough to endure back-to-back blows, while standing in the middle of a storm? Is it truly UNSHAKABLE?*

# *You've Got to be HUNGRY*

Murphy's law states, "Anything that can go wrong will, and at the worst possible time." I don't know who the hell Murphy is, but I can tell you that he, and his law, showed up in a BIG way! While my faith for my healing was stronger than ever, the rest of my life was crashing and burning right before my very eyes!

While enduring 338 radiation seed implants and countless treatments to fight for my health, I was also fighting for my marriage. I then received the life-shattering news that my mother had died of breast cancer. Next, my best friend, Bou who had been a part of my life since the second grade, died while waiting on a liver transplant. All the while, the tremendous emotional and physical stress associated with the cancer continued to put an unbearable strain on my marriage. Despite my deep love for my wife and my desire to make it last forever, our marriage ended in divorce.

The fight for my life, the incredible grief over the deaths of Mama and Bou and the emotional pain and shame of my divorce all seemed to be more than anyone should have to bear. I just *knew* that nothing else could go wrong and I was glad about it because I was barely hanging on. I did my best to take it on the chin, but I could hear the knockout countdown ringing in my soul: *"1, 2, 3... Is he out?"*

No, I wasn't out yet and I thought I'd be able to stand. However, the heavyweight champ, Murphy's Law, had one more blow to deliver: My nationally syndicated talk show was canceled during the worst season of my life! Finally, trying to fight back from life's brutal jabs had worn me out. The public humiliation that came after the loss of my show, combined with the other recent losses, felt way too much to bear.

The heavy blows of life rained down and knocked me senseless. I couldn't think. There was no motivation, no "dusting off my shoulders," no "on to the next goal," no "jumping back up before the referee got to 10!" Life had knocked me down and I was trying to find ways to get back up.

Friends and family who loved and cared about me weren't used to seeing me so groggy and loopy, not being the life of the party. They made vain attempts to encourage me or give me a boost — but to no avail. I just didn't have the strength to move. I was tired of fighting life and I felt empty inside. I felt ashamed, powerless, worthless, and weak. I allowed all my negative self-talk and the voices of outside critics to inundate my mind. My **Unshakable Faith** was, indeed, shaken.

## *All it takes is a Spark*

It is the great Willie Jolley who first said, "A setback is a setup, for a comeback!" Everything in my life was going wrong at that time, as is sometimes the case in life. That's why one of my favorite quotes is: "When things go wrong, don't go with them!"

No matter how much we would like to avoid it, none of us are immune to the sometimes harsh realities of life. As sure as there are twenty-four hours in a day, you will lose things, money, and people. There is no question that your faith will be tested, and you will take some hits. After all, how can you have a **test**imony without a **test?** However, the most powerful element in the equation is how you deal with your adversities. How you handle your test will be the determining factor in your level of greatness!

You can either handle your circumstances or you can let your circumstances handle you! Of course, no one can give you a step-by-step guide on how to successfully handle your circumstances. But I can tell the one thing you certainly want to avoid: Don't even bother asking the question, "Why me?" The Universe is likely to retort back, "Why not you? Who else would you suggest? Would you like to send us some recommendations?"

Here's a second thing you want to avoid: Going around telling people about your troubles. Eighty percent of people don't care, and twenty percent are glad that it's happening to you and not them! HUNGRY people live life from the inside out, not the outside in. It took me some time to re-establish myself in these truths, but I was eventually guided back.

I remember having a conversation during that time with my youngest son, John Leslie. He came into my room and asked, "Daddy, are you going to die from cancer?"

Taking a break from my nothingness, I turned to answer him. "All of us are going to die one day, John Leslie."

"But are you gonna die from *this* without putting up a fight?" He looked at me intently with his big, brown eyes piercing my soul.

"Why do you ask that?"

"Because you're not yourself! You keep the shades down

locked away in this room, in the dark. And it's very quiet in here. You're not listening to your motivational messages anymore. You're not reading anymore..."

I could hear the fear, pain and disappointment in his little voice. It jarred me with deep conviction. "Yes, I'm going to fight. I'm going to live."

Satisfied with my answer, he turned and left the room.

The thing about faith is, even in the gloomiest valley, the slightest glimmer of hope can spark a flame. It can guide you from the darkness back into the light, setting the stage for you to snatch victory from the jaws of defeat! Even though my shades were still drawn, it was a little brighter in the room after he walked out. There was a tiny light in me once again — another glint of hope. I wanted to fight and I was determined to keep my commitment to him to live.

I was staying with my daughter, Ona Brown, at that time. It was Ona who began to feed me mentally and encourage my faith. Ona helped me to start purposely working on myself again. She helped me get back to the place where I was able to believe and see myself beyond cancer. Ona has since written a book entitled, *Are You Angels Unemployed?* I encourage you to read it. She was truly one of my most active angels during that time and remains so today!

I eventually regained enough strength to start reading and studying on my own. I even started listening to my old messages. I began seeing the light at the end of the tunnel. I didn't see myself as a cancer patient any longer, but as a messenger of hope and a catalyst of action, impacting millions of people's lives.

The painful blows that life had dealt me were no match for my faith once it was restored. Murphy didn't win after all. I had a new **Unshakeable Faith** and I felt **unstoppable!**

## *Unstoppable people*

As a kid, I always followed my mother around, watching her very keenly. Mama provided food for us, even if she herself couldn't eat. She'd nibble on saltine crackers to fight off her hunger while giving us a full meal. I remember seeing her sit at the table with only a glass of water during meals. When I would ask her if she was going to eat, she would tell me that she had already eaten.

## *You've Got to be HUNGRY*

I learned from my mother that *sometimes you have to feed your dream before you feed your body!* It was Mamie Brown's dream to be a mother. She was so dedicated to her dream that she would go to bed hungry to feed her HUNGER! Let me say that again, in case you missed it — *she went to bed hungry, so she could feed her HUNGER!*

> *What are you willing to give up? What are you willing to sacrifice? What are you willing to go through for your dream? Greatness comes with a heavy price tag!*

HUNGRY people are willing to pay the price! One of the major lessons I learned from studying my mother was to be unstoppable and relentless in pursuit of whatever it is that you want. Even though she had to work for people like Ms. Harris, despite having to endure discrimination, injustice and humiliation, Mama was unstoppable! Despite the challenges or situations, they may face, people who are *unstoppable* look for solutions, not excuses!

# The Greatness Within to Win

*The average person goes to work and does just enough to keep from being fired, but an unstoppable person, a HUNGRY person, does more than they get paid for.*

When my mother worked for people, they continued to use her services because she was excellent in all she did. She cooked so well that you had to take your shoes off to eat her food — so you could wiggle your toes! She cleaned very thoroughly, and the children of her employers loved her. Mama took care of other people's children, so she'd be able to provide for her own. She made herself invaluable to her employers so she could underwrite her own dream!

I grew up with an understanding that I must approach everything with that type of energy. I believe in this entrepreneurship era that's the kind of mindset we all must-have. I remember being a salesperson in the men's department at Sears. Though I was consistently the top salesperson, they would not promote me because they said it would "lower morale" since I was Colored. "Be a team player and teach the other salespeople to do what you do" those were the instructions my managers gave to me. I did as I was instructed and then they promoted my trainees over me. People that I taught became my bosses!

**Just in case you haven't been told yet, life is not fair.**
**It's not fair that birds eat worms, but they do!**

Them not promoting me didn't matter to me though because, in my mind, I was not working for them. I was training myself for my greatness. They thought they were utilizing me, but I was using them to sharpen my skills. They were basically paying me to learn!

They said promoting me would lower morale: *I wonder how losing their top salesman was for "morale"? **(laugh)*** Once I learned all I could, I moved onto another opportunity. Sears refused to promote me, so I promoted myself right on out of there! My HUNGER promoted me!

**HUNGRY people know that man's rejection is often**

**GOD's redirection!**

It was after leaving Sears that I began working with Mr. Sam Axelrod, the Jewish man who taught me about the *Never Again* mantra. When we worked together, sometimes I would get angry passing by the signs that read, "Jews, Dogs, and Coloreds Not Allowed." Those same signs had been taunting me my entire life, screaming loudly: *"ACCESS DENIED! REJECTION! YOU'RE NOT GOOD ENOUGH!"*

As minorities, Sam and I both understood the pain of racism and discrimination. But Mr. Axelrod taught me a powerful lesson about life through those signs. One day as we traveled, I expressed my anger to Sam. He turned and looked at me intently, and spoke these words:

**"Anger is a wind that blows out the lamp of the mind. Focus all your energy on being a better person so you can become successful, no matter what the signs say."**

As is often said, opportunity often comes disguised as adversity. Leaving Sears to work with Sam turned out to be a tremendous growth opportunity — both as a salesman and a human being. Sam took a special interest in me and began to teach me many things. Sam taught me that to live life on my terms, my intrinsic will would have to be stronger than the adversities I would inevitably face.

# You've Got to be HUNGRY

*In life, you must be more determined than those who will try to hold you down! That was true then and is still true today!*

## Make Moves Not Excuses!

There were many times that I had to feed on the lessons that I learned from Mama and Sam. I had to be relentless, unstoppable and create my own life! I remember one of those times very clearly.

After some measurable success as a first time DJ in Miami, I went to the owner and asked him for a raise. However, Mr. Kline didn't just say no. He said, *"HELL NO!"* I've learned in life never to tolerate being undervalued so I promoted myself out of there too! I ended up taking an offer to work for another radio station, WVKO, all the way in Columbus, Ohio.

It paid more money, which I greatly needed since my wife was pregnant with our second child. Unfortunately, I had to leave her and my son behind so I could travel ahead and get situated. It was my first time ever flying on a plane or traveling out of the state. I certainly did not know what I was in for! I left Miami in December with one suit, no winter coat, no car and only forty dollars in my pocket. The night I arrived in Ohio, I quickly realized that my little brown suit was no match for the Ohio wind chill and that I had no clue what a real winter was!

The forty dollars I left home with didn't last very long. Thankfully, for the first few days, the station's program director, Bill Moss, invited me to stay at his house. However, it was going to be two weeks before I got paid and I needed to make other arrangements. One morning during breakfast after a couple of days with him, I asked Bill if he would be so kind as to loan me seventy-five dollars. I explained to him that I needed it for food and a cheap motel room, just until I got paid.

Since Bill had been kind enough to allow me to stay with him for a few days and we would be working together, I just *knew* that he would understand my position and help me. His response to my request quickly proved me wrong. "Les, the bank and I have a deal. They won't play music and I won't make loans. Good luck, friend!" He then walked away, cracking up, quite amused at his clever response!

His response was truly hard to bear. I was in quite a predicament. The radio station was twelve miles outside of Columbus in the middle of a big field. There was literally nothing around the station for at least three miles. My show was the last one to air each day and at the end of my shift, the building would be locked. Since I didn't have a car, my options were very limited.

With nowhere to go, I decided to hide behind the building and wait until everybody left for the night. When I was sure that no one was watching, I climbed into the large garbage bin that was on the side of the building. I created a little padding made of cardboard boxes, on top of the garbage. I then covered myself with my suit jacket and some newspapers.

Neither, of course, offered much protection against the Ohio winter, but I knew my family was back in Miami counting on me. Despite the freezing temperatures, I stayed there. I was both figuratively and literally HUNGRY! Just like Mama went to bed hungry to feed her HUNGER, I went to my garbage bin bed, hungry and cold, for my dream!

**I'm here to tell you that your dream can keep you warm!**

That garbage bin became my "cheap motel" for the next two weeks. My dream became my electric blanket. I didn't focus on the smell of the trash. I didn't focus on how embarrassed I'd be if anyone found me in the dumpster. I just focused on my dream and on creating the life I wanted! You might be going through a tough time right now too. Don't focus on that.

*Where focus goes, energy flows.* **Hold onto the vision of what it is that you want. Think about it, both night and day. Say to yourself,** *"No matter how bad it is, or how bad it may get, I'm going to make it!"*

Today, I rest comfortably in my own bed or any hotel of my choosing! But when I think of all the uncomfortable places I've slept, I laugh to myself. I've slept in my car, a garbage bin, on my office floor, and on various couches over the years. I've even had to hide in the closet when the janitor came to clean. I've washed up in office buildings when I had no shower. All because I chose to be UNSTOPPABLE!

*Unstoppable people make a way, when there is no way!*

## *You've Got to be HUNGRY*

At first, I was angry when Bill refused to help me. But you know what? He really did me a favor! He stirred up more of the GOD-force in me called HUNGER! I was HUNGRY to make it, so I did!

***HUNGRY people don't make excuses; they make moves! HUNGRY people figure things out!***

Mama and Sam taught me how to be *unstoppable*. They taught me how to move in **Unshakable Faith**! You must become a risk-taker in life. You must operate outside of your comfort zone. The HUNGER in your heart must be greater than the hunger in your belly!

Challenge yourself! Stretch yourself! Push yourself! Facedown your fears! An airplane can't fly without the resistance of air. You can't learn good horsemanship by riding a tame horse. You can't make lemonade with sugar alone; you've got add some sour lemons. But the harder the battle, the sweeter the victory!

***You are more powerful than you give yourself credit for so be Unstoppable. Move-in Unshakable Faith. Be HUNGRY!***

# The Greatness Within to Win

During our time together, each day, Mr. Sam Axelrod would share with me his quote for the day. I can still remember some of my favorite ones:

*"This is a usable world, and if you don't use it in the right way, it's a cruel world."*

*"All of us are self-made, but only the successful will admit it."* **Earl Nightingale**

*"Always strive to get on top in life because the bottom is overcrowded."*

*"Leslie, GOD created you, but YOU create your life*

***Always remember, UNSTOPPABLE PEOPLE, don't allow negative circumstances, injustice, tragedy, or lack to define them! They define themselves and create the life they want!***

**Chapter 4: A Window for my New House**

# Chapter Four

# A Window for My New House

## NOW Urgency

## *Now Urgency*

S ome years ago, I told my mother that I wanted to buy her a home. Apparently, I was not moving fast enough to satisfy my mother's timeline. One day I arrived home to see a single, used window propped up against a wall in the living room. When I saw it, I said, "Mama, what is this?" My mama went on to explain to me it was a window that had been salvaged from a home that was demolished in the neighborhood she lived in. She must've seen it in passing, lying there in a heap of rubble waiting to be discarded, and asked someone to retrieve it for her.

I remember laughing so hard when she explained her reasoning behind it. She said, "Now when you buy me a house, you won't have to buy windows for the whole house because we'll have this one already." As funny as it sounds though, that window being present created a sense of urgency in me. Every time I walked past it, I was pushed to get that house for my mother.

*Have you ever thought of something you wanted to do so badly, but you just felt the time wasn't right?*

## *You've Got to be HUNGRY*

You may be experiencing this right now. You've built a logical, practical case in your mind for why this is not the time to move forward on your idea, thought or situation. Well, guess what? Sometimes being logical and practical about your goals is the best way to ensure that they never ignite! Commit to living your life where you are right *now* with what you have right *now*! Always be willing to keep pushing forward. Live in the present and make as much impact as you possibly can, while you can. It is George Washington Carver who said:

**"Do what you can, where you are, what you have**
**and never be satisfied."**

When my mother had the chance to adopt me and my brother, she didn't wait for "the right time." She operated with a sense of **NOW Urgency**. She wanted me to operate in that same sense of urgency when it came to buying her a home! Whatever your dream to do, *DO IT NOW!*

## You Can't Get Out of Life Alive

They say life is like a vapor. We are here only for a brief time then we're gone. We've all heard it: "Life is short." But I don't believe life is short. I believe too many people take too long to decide to live! For as beautiful and magnificent as life can be, none of us know how long we have on earth. We all know the adage that tells us to, "Live each day as if it's your last because one day it will be." Truer words have rarely been spoken. Unfortunately, many of us do not take heed to this warning.

I always admired the work and words of renowned author and speaker, Dr. Wayne Dyer. Wayne and I had both worked hard over the years to raise money for the support of PBS. We had a mutual friend named Lynne Kitchen who knew of our shared love for PBS. She also knew that Wayne and I had both been mentored by a man named Jack Boland- a giant in the self-development industry.

Lynne had an amazing idea for the two of us to collaborate on a live special. The idea was groundbreaking, two titans of public television coming together and jointly producing a PBS special that would raise millions of dollars! Wayne and I were both eager to produce the show, but with both of our schedules being so busy, it was hard to coordinate a time to meet. As people tend to do, we kept putting it off. The project was pushed to the back burner for several months.

One day, Wayne called to tell me that he was coming to Orlando so we could finally sit down and "ink the deal." Wayne and I had so many similarities in terms of what we had experienced in life. I was excited about connecting with him and about planning the special together. What we were aspiring to do was truly unprecedented! However, it was a visit and a venture that was never going to happen.

Wayne died in his sleep prior to us being able to connect, just a few days after that phone call. We had allowed other things to take precedence. We didn't "live like we were dying" and, therefore, missed an opportunity to expand our legacies. Needless to say, I was crushed. Dr. Wayne Dyer was a powerful being and I can still see visions of the two of us making history for our beloved PBS. But that is the thing about time — *it truly waits for no one.*

Whatever you want to do, you must do it NOW! Make the move NOW! When you have ideas, goals, and dreams, you must live your life with a strategy of NOW. NOW is the time to walk into your purpose and take charge of your dreams. You must move with what I call "a

NOW sense of urgency." There is no time to wait until all your ducks are in a row. For all you know, there may never be any ducks along your path.

In October of 2014, I was speaking in South Africa. I happened to look across the street from the hotel where I was staying and saw a sign that advertised a relationship seminar. It was being hosted on the same day by Dr. Myles Munroe. I thought, *"Wow, what are the odds that my long-time friend, spiritual brother and I would both be in the same foreign country and city, on the same street, on the same day! "* I was so thrilled to have the chance for an unexpected reunion with Myles.

We had been great friends for many years. He and I had traveled together on private planes, spoken together, shared intimate details of our lives with one another, and grew together as leaders. I even wrote the Foreword for his first book. It had been years since we'd seen each other. I could not wait to see that famous smile and give him a big hug!

I knew Myles would get as huge a kick out of us both being there at the same time, just as I had. I went over to the hotel where his event was being held and introduced myself to his staff. They told me that they already knew who I was. I said, "Great! I'd like to speak with Dr. Myles briefly."

One of his staff responded, "I apologize, Mr. Brown. He's doing a relationship seminar with couples, sir. We cannot interrupt him."

I was quite anxious to get past that point in the conversation. I just wanted to see my friend. "I do understand. But if you let him know that it's *me* who's here, I know he will call me in there or he'll come out here."

She was unwilling to interrupt, but nonetheless eager to find a solution for me. "I'll do something better for you. How about I set you up to have breakfast with him tomorrow morning before he leaves?"

I felt something in my spirit telling me to push my request to see him that day, but I reluctantly agreed to the breakfast meeting. Despite the nagging feeling that continued, I talked myself out of insisting that his staff go tell him I was there. I took for granted that we would have breakfast the next morning. I convinced myself that would be a better opportunity because he and I could talk at greater length. However, something in me was saying, "Do it NOW!"

# The Greatness Within to Win

*Have you ever had the experience of not listening to your heart? I was soon to face the regret of that moment...*

I arrived early that next morning, excited to see my friend. The lady who had set up the breakfast came out to me with a look of grave disappointment. "I'm so sorry, Mr. Brown, but he left earlier than expected."

I was instantly filled with disheartenment. I would never again have an opportunity to connect with my friend, Dr. Myles Munroe. Just a few weeks later he and his wife, along with some members of his staff, all died in a plane crash. I was so angry with myself and GOD! I couldn't believe I'd missed my chance to see my friend again, *forever*.

People who are HUNGRY know that tomorrow is not promised and they live like it! Dr. Myles Munroe wrote over sixty books and was arguably one of the most intelligent and powerful ministers on the planet, and I'm grateful to have had the honor to call him my friend.

In an instant, he was gone! The beautiful thing about Myles Munroe is that he lived every day like it was his last. In everything he did and in every message he gave, he made it known that his goal was to "die empty." He encouraged us to "rob the cemetery" by pouring everything we have into our dreams and our lives until there is nothing left.

We all have a season when we are required to give everything we have to our purpose. That is what both Dr. Wayne Dyer and Dr. Myles Munroe did. They lived their lives with a strategy of NOW. They knew that we all have an expiration date. Even though no one knows when that date is, it is up to you to make your mark on this side of your expiration date! You must make a conscious decision to give life everything you've got while you are here. Time is irreplaceable and you can't get out of life alive. So please, *DO IT NOW!*

## *Not Just Now, But RIGHT NOW!*

I am still haunted by the voice of LaKeisha, an aspiring young singer whom I'd met while I was living in the Washington, D.C. area. This is the story...

One day my phone rang. When I answered, a woman on the other end said, "Hello, Mr. Brown! I understand that you will be speaking at a church in the D.C. area in the coming weeks and I would like to know if my daughter can come and open for you by singing?"

I was a little surprised and responded, "Maybe, but I've never heard your daughter sing."

The lady spoke no words in response. Instead, she confidently put her daughter on the phone. LaKeisha started singing and, right away, I knew she had star power! This young lady's voice sounded like a mixture of Whitney Houston with a taste of Patti Labelle! I was blown away to say the least. I immediately decided that not only did I want her to open for me, but I also wanted to make sure her voice was heard all over the world! I allowed her to sing for me on the day of the event and LaKeisha unleashed her gift! The entire congregation was in tears and standing on their feet, as her voice rang through the church, with clarity and beauty. When LaKeisha sang, you knew you were in the presence of greatness. We all marveled at her voice.

As soon as I left the church, I called a friend of mine who is a record producer. I told him that he had to get LaKeisha in the studio ASAP to record and be signed with him. Sly trusted my judgment, so the next day, she was in his studio. He called me later that evening to report. "Man, Brown! You were right about her; she is the one! Not only can she sing, but she can write too. The lyrics just flow out of her!" I was ecstatic! I couldn't wait to hear the recording. The day she met him in the studio was a Monday. I assumed they'd be recording that day, so I called the next day to ask for a copy of what they'd done. Sly informed me that he hadn't recorded their session yet because LaKeisha was going on a brief trip. She told Sly she'd be back on Wednesday and would come in to record as soon as she returned.

On that Thursday, I was again eager to hear the recording. However, my excitement quickly faded when I heard the voicemail that Sly left me. The voicemail was full of panic, instructing me to call him back. When I called, he answered and said, without any warning or explanation, "She's dead. She died, Les." He told me that she was in the car with her boyfriend who had fallen asleep at the wheel. LaKeisha died in a car wreck before she ever made it back to record that session.

***William Shatner has a song, with lyrics that say,
"Live like you're gonna die because you're gonna."[7]
Whatever you want to do in life, You Must Do It
Now!***

124

I am still devastated to this day. LaKeisha had resigned from her teaching job and was ready to pursue her dream of singing full-time. She died with the right intentions in her heart. Nonetheless, because she never recorded herself, we'll never have a chance to hear her powerful voice. LaKeisha was moving in the now, but not the *RIGHT NOW!*

I'm reminded of a lady that I recently met who became one of the essential people to help me complete this book project. Like I mentioned previously, **"Whatever you're seeking, is also seeking you".** Laneen Haniah, who goes by *Dr. Intimacy*, was in town on vacation when we met. There was somewhere else that she was "supposed to be" the night we met, but as she tells it, in her spirit she knew she needed to cancel those plans and stay where she was.

Laneen was with a very good mutual friend, film producer Ric Mathis, who was taking her around town to network with some people. After a full day together and having already made some great connections, she had the option to stay with Ric or go to the location where she was scheduled to be interviewed on a local influencer's Facebook Live broadcast. She was excited about recording the broadcast because it was her last chance, before leaving town, to get any type of media exposure.

But something in her heart was saying, "This is not what GOD has for you. You didn't come to Atlanta for this." Laneen decided to listen. She didn't know in her mind what was going to happen, but she trusted her heart's inner *knowing.* She had no idea at the time that Ric is like family to me or that he intended to stop by my house. She simply said, 'YES' to her heart by faith. Much to her surprise, she soon ended up in the living room of Les Brown!

Once they arrived, I decided within three minutes of speaking to this woman that I wanted to interview her on my Facebook Live. I had no idea that she had canceled a scheduled Facebook Live broadcast with someone else! I think her HUNGER was speaking to my HUNGER, telling us what needed to happen. Within hours, the video we recorded together had over 20,000 views, the most-viewed Facebook Live video she had ever participated in.

Dr. Intimacy got the media coverage she desired and I was about to get what I wanted as well. After further conversation, I learned that Laneen owns a publishing company that specializes in working with public speakers and incredible humans who have incredible stories. I was ecstatic when I found out because finishing this book had become an obsession for me at that time. Thinking about this book was keeping me up at night; twenty-one years was as long as I wanted to wait for this project to be completed and I was HUNGRY to get it out!

Laneen moved with a sense of **NOW Urgency**. This type of work is her passion and she wasn't going to gamble with this opportunity. She was willing to change her entire schedule around for a stranger to answer the call on her life and now she is part of a project that will impact billions of lives worldwide!

*Some people say that opportunity knocks on every door, but I don't believe that it knocks. I believe that it stands silently by, waiting to be recognized.*

We must realize that tomorrow is not promised. Whatever it is that you are called to do, DO IT NOW. Move with a sense of **NOW Urgency,** toward your **Heart-Centered** dreams and goals, with **Unshakeable Faith!** Learn to discern the difference between the essential and the non-essential, the things that can wait and the things that CANNOT!

# *You've Got to be HUNGRY*

Sometimes life will teach us things the hard way. If we are blessed enough to live through those hard lessons, we have another chance to get it right! I challenge you to take an assessment of the things you are putting off until "the right time." Assess where you may be stuck "living your life inside of your head" versus out loud and in action.

We all remember Michael Jackson's celebrated promotion of his *This Is It* concert, which was to be his last concert. But it never happened. After years of planning and various delays, he was finally ready for his farewell tour. Instead, we ended up saying farewell to him. The world was devastated when he died before he ever stepped on stage for a single show.

*Time truly waits for no one. Opportunity waits for no one. Operate in NOW URGENCY. You must "Live each day as if it were your last because one day, it will be."*

Reflect on your goals and dreams. Write down five things that you want to do that you have not accomplished yet. It may be pursuing a new career path.

It could be taking up that hobby you have always dreamed of. It may be traveling to a certain place on the globe. Maybe there is a person that you have been trying to muster up the courage to reconcile with or one who you have been trying to find the strength to walk away from! Maybe you want to write a book or move to your dream location.

There is *something* that will cause your heart to flutter! Drop this book, running from the house barefoot if necessary, and DO IT NOW. Whatever it is, do it with a sense of urgency — **Do It *RIGHT NOW!***

## <u>*Just Keep on Living!*</u>

As has been clearly illustrated, we all must prepare for the unsettling unpredictability of death. It often appears unexpectedly, and we never seem to be quite "ready" when our loved ones go. But what about people who *want* to die? According to statistics, published by Charts Bin[8]:

- There are approximately one million suicides committed worldwide, each year.

- Every 40 seconds somebody dies by suicide.

- There has been a 60% increase in worldwide suicide rates in the last 45 years.

- There are 20 failed suicide attempts for each successful one, meaning every 40 seconds 21 people attempt suicide and 1 succeeds.

As I stated in the introduction: *"Those of us who have been exposed to toxic and mentally debilitating programming— programming that has been unrelentingly instilled in us over decades, and reinforced on every level of life — can't just be told, 'Be positive and enthusiastic; have a burning desire and you can live your dream!'"*

People like that have given up somewhere on the inside. A friend of mine has a quote that says, **"There are many people whose ears have gone deaf to motivational words; whose souls have become numb to encouragement."** These are the ones who feel helpless, hopeless and powerless.

I remember an occasion when a dear friend of mine, who I will call "John," was going through a very difficult season of his life. John's wife had filed for divorce and wanted him to leave their home. I knew that John was feeling down and I was certainly concerned about him. Since I was unable to get to his location, I contacted a mutual friend of ours and asked him to go over and check on John. I explained that he was going through a rough time and that I didn't think he should be alone.

The mutual friend went over to spend time with John and I felt relieved knowing that someone was there with him. I felt that I had done enough and that John would be fine. Much to my dismay, our mutual friend called me back not long afterward somewhat frantic. He had stepped out for less than fifteen minutes to go to the store, and upon his return, he was unable to get in contact with John. John's car was present, but he would not answer the door or his phone.

Later that day, John's wife returned home. When she opened the closet door to hang up her coat, she discovered her husband's cold, dead body. He had hung himself and ended his own life. I knew that John was depressed, but I didn't realize how hopeless he was really feeling. I never thought that he would be "the type to commit suicide." That incident haunted me for many years. I wished I had kept John on the phone and talked him out of that dark place. Something in my heart felt like I could have done more.

The truth is, I don't know if I could have saved John. However, I do believe that I can save someone now by sharing what I learned from this tragedy that personally touched my life. **Don't take your mental health for granted! Don't take the mental health of your loved ones for granted!** When your mental health is threatened, you need to address it — not just *now*, but *RIGHT NOW!* When you observe someone around you who appears to be suffering from any kind of mental health struggle, you need to address it, not just *now,* but *RIGHT NOW!*

I believe we are way past the stage of being able to judge who seems like "the type to commit suicide." In September of 2019, a prominent megachurch pastor by the name of Jarrid Wilson committed suicide. For many years, Pastor Wilson was a forerunner for addressing mental health in the church and spoke openly about his long-time struggle with depression and suicidal thoughts. Wilson led the charge in helping people overcome depression and suicidal thoughts. According to reports, he helped tens of thousands of people choose to live. He surely didn't seem like "the type to commit suicide."

*If you feel depressed, anxious or suicidal, please don't ignore the signs. Talk to someone, reach out for help, RIGHT NOW. If someone around you seems hopeless and in despair, don't assume they'll get past it. Reach out to them, RIGHT NOW. Make them get help, even if they don't think they need it!*

One statistic shows that every twelve minutes someone commits suicide in the United States — totaling 129 people each day and 47,173 deaths per year — making suicide the tenth leading cause of death. Death by suicide outnumbers death by homicide, by a two-to-one ratio! The types of people who commit suicide vary, from children as young as six years old, all the way to senior citizens in their 80s.

Recently, a single mother drove to the Homestead Grays Bridge in Pennsylvania. She parked her car on the bridge and got out, leaving her three small children inside. She walked a short distance away and jumped to her death. Another incident occurred where a mom walked into her children's bedroom, only to find her six-year-old daughter had killed herself. She fastened one end of a belt around her neck and the other end to a crib — this was after being sent to her room for misbehaving! From those who have suffered harrowing tragedies to those who seem to have it all together, from the rich to the poor, from the average Joe to the most famous celebrities— people of every race, religion, and creed — every human being is potentially "the type to commit suicide"!

*There is no "type" any longer. Suicide, depression and mental illness are on a rampage, targeting anyone who doesn't take their threat seriously!*

Due to the tragedies of life, due to many uncertainties and our volatile, stressful environment, people often live in fear. We live in fear of rejection, fear of loneliness, fear of poverty, fear of chronic disease, fear of accidents, fear of domestic terror, fear of natural disasters, fear of government wars, and fear of economic collapses — just to name a few! A record number of people are experiencing anxiety, depression, and sleeplessness. There are anxiety triggers all around us.

I believe the fact of the matter is that there is no one who is not suffering from at least some degree of mental illness or emotional disturbance. I have never heard anyone say that before, but I believe it with all my heart. Your sense of **NOW Urgency** must be most critically applied in the area of taking care of your mental health and emotional stability. It must be most critically applied, regarding watching over those who are around you — your children, your significant other, your family, and your close friends.

I have had more than my fair share of challenging situations. I could have easily allowed fear to lead my decisions. Thankfully, I grew into the understanding of knowing that fear, as Zig Ziglar said, is only "**F**alse **E**vidence **A**ppearing **R**eal." I am here to tell you that suicide is not the answer! Since erected in 1937, 1,700 people have jumped from the Golden Gate Bridge, with 25 who survived. One of the survivors, Kevin Hines, said, "The moment I hit free-fall was an instant regret — I recognized that I made the greatest mistake in my life. I said to myself, what have I done? I don't want to die. GOD, please save me!"

*No matter how bad it seems, don't make a permanent decision-based on temporary circumstances!*
*As bad as life is today, it can be just as good tomorrow.*

I remember there was a time in my life when I was homeless, sleeping on the floor of my office. During that time, I traveled through Detroit and needed somewhere to stay. A friend of a friend, who was a stranger to me, allowed me to sleep on his couch. He was a wealthy doctor who had previously heard some of my messages. Before I left, he handed me $95,000 in cash. When I asked him what it was for, he said that I made him laugh after his mother died and that he believed whatever it was that I had planned for my life, I'd be a success at it!

I turned that $95,000 into 1.5 million in just under a year! I'm telling you — *just keep on living!* Just like life can bring unexpected tragedy, it can bring unexpected blessings and favor, as well. Just like you can go through a season when everything that can go wrong does, you can also go through a season when everything that can go right does! You must walk in your *Unshakeable Faith* and say to yourself, *"Just keep on living!"*

As my mentor, Sam Axelrod used to say to me, **"GOD created you, but you create your life!"** Create a life that inspires you to *just keep on living*. Yes, some terrible things may happen that will be out of your control, but you get to control your HUNGER. Every beautiful tree was once a seed buried in the dirt. When life buries you, don't see it as an invitation to the grave; see it as the soil that is fertilizing your greatness!

*Create beauty around you by loving others. If your life seems dark, find someone whose life is darker than yours and be his or her light. You can't make someone else feel better without feeling better yourself!*

When interviewed, Kevin Hines said that as he was headed to jump off the bridge, he was hoping for just one glimmer of hope along the way. He said that if one person had been kind to him, recognized him or even just smiled at him, he would have turned around. You must understand that you always have value to someone. Your children need your love, your smile and your time. Your significant other needs your encouragement and validation. There is somebody on your job that needs you to take the time to listen to them. There is someone at your church who feels hopeless; they need your hug. There is a neighbor who feels forgotten; they need your company. Someone in your family needs your forgiveness and a second chance. *A stranger needs your smile.*

The bottom line is this: **The only way you can make a difference is to *be here*; so, you must find a way to do just that!** When you are HUNGRY for your dreams, it consumes you. You won't have the energy or time to nurture depression when you are focused on becoming the next greatest version of yourself! *You've Got to Be HUNGRY to just keep on living!*

# The Greatness Within to Win

## DON'T QUIT

*When things go wrong as they sometimes will,*
*When the road you're trudging seems all*
*uphill, When the funds are low, and the debts*
*are high And you want to smile, but you have*
*to sigh, When care is pressing you down a bit,*
*Rest if you must, but don't you quit.*

*Life is strange with its twists and*
*turns As every one of us sometimes*
*learns And many a failure comes*
*about*
*When he might have won had he stuck it out;*

*Don't give up though the pace seems slow—*
*You may succeed with another blow.*
*Success is failure turned inside*
*out— The silver tint of the clouds*
*of doubt,*

*And you never can tell just how close you*
*are, It may be near when it seems so far;*
*So, stick to the fight when you're hardest hit—*
*It's when things seem worst that you must not*
*quit.*

*~by John Greenleaf Whittier~*

# You've Got to be HUNGRY

*The best cure for depression is to get your mind off what has you down and on what can lift others up. Instead of thinking about dying, you can be the reason that someone else decides to live!*

*Embrace life with a sense of NOW URGENCY!*

**Chapter 5: Make the Shoe Fit**

# Chapter Five

# Make the Shoe Fit

# Grow Continuously

There is a saying that goes, "If the shoe fits, wear it." But Mamie Brown lived by a different saying: "If the shoe don't fit, make it fit!" I remember at Christmas time, Mama bringing home hand-me-down clothes from the families she worked for. One Christmas, she brought home some nice leather shoes from one of the families whose son wore a size eight. Unfortunately, that was a half size too small for me. When I tried the shoes on, I couldn't get my feet into them because they were not big enough.

When I told Mama that I couldn't fit them, I figured that would be the end of it. However, Mama called my sister, Margaret Ann, and told her to run some warm water in the bathtub and to bring her some Vaseline. My sister did as she was told. As the water was running, Mama began rubbing my feet with Vaseline. She then stuffed my feet into those too-small shoes! I was instructed to get into the tub of water and walk around. "And you better not splash any water on the floor while you walking either!" Mama said.

I didn't know what the point was, so after walking

around in the tub for a little while, I called to Mama to let her know that the shoes still didn't fit. But she answered back, "Walk until they do!" I walked backward and forwards for what seemed like forever. However, much to my surprise, after so many laps in the tub, the water-soaked leather became a comfortable eight and a half — *just my size!*

If it were up to me, I would have just given up on having those nice leather shoes because they didn't fit me. I did not know they could be *stretched* into a perfect fit! It reminds me of how people treat their dreams and goals. Many people refuse to stretch themselves because they feel they *don't fit* the requirements or cannot measure up to the demands of what it will take to get there. The truth of the matter is, without trying, you will never know what you can or cannot do.

No matter what you think you know, you don't know enough about yourself to doubt your own abilities. According to the laws of aerodynamics, a bumblebee isn't supposed to be able to fly because its puny, little wings are not designed to hold up its large body. It's a good thing for bumblebees that they never studied aerodynamics and don't know of their ill-designed bodies.

Despite what science says, they continue to fly anyway! Sometimes you need to be *intelligently ignorant*. When you are targeted to be the victim of policies, politics, religions, cultures, and environments that are stacked against you — systems put in place and intentionally designed to destroy your sense of self — you must be like the bumblebee.

Like those shoes, you must **Grow Continuously!** There will be times in your life when you feel that you can't overcome the odds. However, when you continue to work on yourself and develop mental resolve, increase your skills and surround yourself with nourishing relationships, you will be able to defeat whatever obstacles life throws your way! Walk those laps around the tub of life until the shoe fits! Don't allow your circumstances to define who you are; create the circumstances you want for yourself! Stretch yourself until you fit the occasion and meet the requirements!

## Standing in A Wheelchair

I've listened to hundreds of motivational messages repeatedly to expand my mind, to raise my own bar, to challenge myself to reach beyond my comfort zone. Why?

145

# You've Got to be HUNGRY

Because I know to *have something you've never had before, you have to become someone you've never been before! There is no way to know when all of the motivation that I've filled myself up with will be put to the test of application.* But trust me, those tests *always* come!

One day, my son, Patrick, was pushing me in a wheelchair through the airport. It was the first time that I'd been in public not being able to walk. As you can probably imagine, I was embarrassed. I hung my head down, hoping that people would not recognize me, but many did and greeted me warmly. I tried to hide my feelings, but their facial expressions showed me that they felt sorry for me or maybe they just wanted to ask what happened.

Amidst my embarrassment, I paused to ask myself, *"Why are you ashamed that the people you're going to speak to will know your condition?"*

I realized that I needed to grow and stretch myself for this new challenge and I certainly rose to the occasion. Even though I spoke from a wheelchair on stage, I received a *standing ovation* from the audience. It really encouraged me to know that people did not judge me because of my condition. They were focused on my message, and although I could not physically stand up, I stood up through all of them when I received their ovation! My HUNGER stood up in me and in them. I was told later that some people felt I was moving so much in the wheelchair they were nervous that I would fall out. *(laugh)*

You must realize that things are going to happen to you in life — things that you can't even begin to imagine. It doesn't really matter what happens to you; what matters most is how you deal with it! I no longer need a wheelchair to get around, but even if I did, I would not hang my head down. I will always hold my head up high! I should have

never cared about the stares of the people looking with their questioning expressions because I realize in that experience, there was an opportunity for me to *Grow Continuously*. That is true for every experience, no matter how uncomfortable or humiliating.

*Do NOT ever again, let people — whether for you or against you — determine your level of growth and greatness! It's up to you to Grow Continuously in every situation.*

# You've Got to be HUNGRY

## You Either Expand or You Are Expendable

To build my speaking business, I made so many calls that, at one time, I had a callous on my ear. People thought it was a big mole! I made over 100 calls a day. I even made calls on the weekends, when businesses were closed, just in case somebody was doing overtime. Lo and behold, one day somebody answered the phone. It was on a Sunday afternoon that I met my first corporate client!

Just like Mamie Brown told everyone she knew that she wanted to raise a child, I had a dream to do corporate training. As I was going through my list of contacts, I methodically dialed the number of the Michigan Bell corporate office. Someone picked up and I greeted the person saying, "Hello. My name is Les Brown! I'm a motivational speaker. Do you, or someone you know, need a speaker to come in and motivate the salespeople to increase their performance?"

In a voice of bewilderment, the person on the other end asked, "Do you know this is Sunday afternoon?"

I responded with just as much confidence, as he spoke with bewilderment. "Yes, I do!" I thought to myself, *"if somebody is in on the weekend working, just like I do, that would be the person I needed to talk to!"* He told me to come in the next morning so we could speak face-to-face and that's how I landed my first corporate contract! I trained Michigan Bell employees, Illinois Bell, Sprint, and AT&T — all because I was willing to do the things that others won't do!

No matter what your passion or your dream is, you will have to learn to master it. A recent book came out that says, "average is over!" It will take time and demanding work, but the question is: Will you one day look back in regret or in delight for how you handled your dreams? Maybe it seems extreme, making 100 calls a day, to the point of a calloused ear. You know what? It was extreme! I missed out on time with friends and family. I missed out on rest. I missed out on recreation, but that's what it took for the reward that I enjoy today. I don't regret what I missed. I delight in what I've gained, and how I've impacted the lives of billions of people around the world.

Make no mistake about it. If you're not growing, you're shrinking! We live in an era that literally operates at lightning speed. If you aren't plugged in, you're left out. Now more than ever, it is critical to constantly reach further and **Grow Continuously**.

# *You've Got to be HUNGRY*

Alvin Toffler, the author of *Future Shock*, made a profound statement. "The illiterate of the twenty-first century will not be those who cannot read and write, but those who cannot learn, unlearn, and relearn." He was right. Change is constant, particularly in this era. Being flexible and willing to **Grow Continuously** are the new basic requirements for success.

Advances in technology allow businesses to move at the speed of light and the direction can change in a millisecond. As the great Robert Schuler said, "We're living in a time where you either expand or you are expendable." You must be nimble enough to ride the waves of change or you will crash and drown. Maybe if I were in that same position today, working to build my speaking business, I'd send out 100 texts a day or make 100 social media connections or set up 100 webinars!

You need to understand what it is going to take to win at what you're pursuing. You must continue to train and educate yourself to remain relevant. *You must Grow Continuously. You've Got to Be HUNGRY!*

## *Sharpening Your Axe*

Abraham Lincoln said, "If I had six hours to chop a tree down, I'd spend four sharpening my axe." The strongest tool you have is your mind. We must constantly sharpen and develop our minds. I agree with America's foremost business philosopher and  writer, Peter Drucker, who said, "This is an era of accelerated change, overwhelming complexity, and tremendous competition, facing us all." In less than a decade, over 47 million jobs will be eliminated in the United States due to the rise of AI (Artificial Intelligence), technology, cheap labor abroad and apps. This is an era in which job security no longer exists. This is the time when you must have the mindset of an entrepreneur, control your own personal economy, create your own jobs, and make your own impact! ***We're coming to the end of work!***

According to the Department of Labor, over 20,000 people lose their jobs every month. I remember my sister, Sharon, coming to me one day to inform me that the company where she'd worked for twenty-two years was downsizing. They were firing her and bringing in a replacement from India. To add insult to her injury, they demanded that my sister train the new employee. She tried to refuse this indignity but then learned that effectively training her replacement was a mandatory requirement for receiving her severance pay.

# *You've Got to be HUNGRY*

After the incident with my sister, it confirmed that the days of the 40/40/40 plan are nearing an end. Working 40 hours a week for 40 years to retire on 40 percent of your income is no longer a realistic plan. Not that it was ever that great of a plan, to begin with, but soon, it won't even be an option! This is the time to ask yourself, *"What is my strategy for being here? What is my next move?"*

Sadly, so many people focus on making a living instead of living their making. Studies show there is a thirty percent increase in heart attacks that occur on Monday mornings. People who are waking up to the grim reality of spending another forty-plus hours at a dreaded job that they despise, often die on the toilet.

*To reduce your risk of a heart attack, you can either stop going to the toilet on Monday mornings, or you can start living the life you desire to live!*

You must **Grow Continuously.** Grow in terms of your talents and skills and every area of your life. Put yourself in a position to get off that dead-end job! As Mamie Brown always said, "Used-to-bees don't make no honey!" Never mind who or what you used to be. *Who and what are you now?* This is the time that you must challenge yourself! This is the time to develop at least three core competencies — three things that you are skilled enough to do to get paid for them. Become the person who can earn a living doing what you love!

Jim Rohn once said, "Work harder on yourself than on your job." In the middle of the most recent economic recession, Warren Buffett was asked what the most important investment was that people should make. This is a man who has made billions of dollars in the stock market and real estate. His answer was: "The most important investment you can make is in yourself." Mr. Buffett was correct! YOU are your greatest asset.

As an asset, you must find ways to appreciate it! Sometimes it is still hard for me to believe that I earn more in one hour than most Americans will earn in an entire year. I don't share this to impress you, but to impress upon you, that:

> **We shouldn't work to get paid by the hour:**
> **We should work to get paid for the value you bring to the hour!**

I want you to understand the power of investing in yourself. ***Knowledge is the new currency.*** Investing in yourself will yield the most profitable ROI! Most of us never use the power that we have because we live in a world where we are told more about our limitations than our potential. This is why we must take the time to invest in our minds. We must acquire the knowledge to expand our vision of ourselves. We must "sharpen our ax," sharpen our thinking and sharpen our skills. We must **Grow Continuously**.

## ***Your Health Is Your Wealth***

I had a very frugal friend. She was always cutting expenses and looking for ways to save money. She kept putting off going to the doctor, saying it would be too expensive. It turns out that she had a treatable illness, which she had taken too long to get checked. She died as a result. However, it wasn't really the disease that killed her. It was the waiting to have it treated! The money that she saved through neglecting her health, she lost it all to the grave.

It is said that the number one healthcare expense is delayed treatment. **Your health is your wealth**, so the first part of continuous growth is TAKING CARE OF YOU! When Howard Hughes, one of the richest men in the world, died, someone asked how much money he had lost in his investments. The answer was given: "All of it. I've never seen a bank riding behind a hearse." Yes, medical care can be costly, but nothing is more costly to your dreams than death!

One of the most important lessons I've learned in life is that we all need to manage our own health and wellness. Work harder on preventing illness than treating it! However, if you do find yourself battling illness, you must have a partnership with the doctors who are treating you. You need to take responsibility for your part in your own healing. Ask a lot of questions and be involved in your care. Don't be so trusting of a doctor's opinion just because they are a doctor.

The fact of the matter is, we need doctors and I greatly appreciate the many health care providers that have been a part of helping me stay alive and healthy. But it is also a fact that we have little to no information on the track record or qualifications of the doctors in charge of our care. Therefore, I highly suggest that when in need of medical care, you do your own research, get someone to help you, and find out and consider all of your options. **Grow Continuously** learning about your health.

Again, I say, *ask questions!* Find out what the side effects of your medications are. Find out if there are options with fewer side effects. Find out if the medications are addictive. You also need to know how your current medications interact with each other, as well as how any new prescriptions will impact your regimen. Also, find out if there are herbal alternatives. According to the FDA, 1.3 million people are harmed annually by medication errors!

Just because someone has a title or has gone through extensive training, it doesn't mean they always know what's best for you. Consider your doctor's advice carefully, but also listen to your loved ones, who know you better than any doctor. They can see things that you and the doctor may miss. So, if something doesn't seem right or your loved ones suggest an alternative, get a second opinion — *a third or fourth, if necessary.* Be willing to explore alternative treatments, as well. I also encourage you to apply any spiritual or religious beliefs you ascribe to. However, when considering "using faith" for your healing, let me remind you that even though Jesus walked on water, He used a boat to get there! Use *everything* available to you — spiritual, traditional and homeopathic treatments — to maintain your wellness.

## *The Greatness Within to Win*

*The bottom line is this: When you're faced with a medical challenge, you're in a partnership with the medical team and YOU ARE THE LEAD PARTNER! Nobody should care more about your life than YOU!*

I don't know what you are facing, but after having 338 radiation seed implants, for prostate cancer and seeing my PSA continue to rise to over 2,400, after learning that cancer had formed masses in seven areas of my body — my doctors told me that my chances for survival were "slim to none." I told them that I'd take "slim". Twenty-seven years later, I'm still here because I was HUNGRY to stay alive! I took care of me. I continued to grow into a person that is committed to staying alive... for as long as I possibly can!

Someone once asked the question: "When is it that a man or woman dies?" The answer was: "When their dreams die when they stop growing when they stop reaching." Don't stop reaching for optimal health. Don't be like my friend who died because she refused to invest in her own physical well-being! While investing in your mind, don't forget about your body and your emotional health. The only way to make sure that your goals and dreams do not die is to stay HUNGRY and STAY ALIVE!

## *<u>Suicide on A Payment Plan</u>*

*You may not struggle with suicidal thoughts, but not taking care of your health is suicide on a payment plan!*

*When is the last time you've had a checkup?* If it's been more than a year, schedule one *today* and get all the required tests to ensure your health!

*Is something hurting on your body or does something seem "Out of Balance"?* Don't ignore it! Get it checked NOW before it's too late to cure what could have been easily treated!

*Are you feeling blue, hopeless or apathetic about life?* If nothing you do seems to improve your outlook and emotional energy, there could be a mental health issue involved. Get some help RIGHT NOW!

*Are you overweight?* It's great to love your body image, no matter what weight you are. However, it's not good to pretend that you're healthy when being overweight is causing issues! Cultivate a new lifestyle and get to your optimal weight, so you can live your optimal life. Yes, love your body the way it is, but love your life enough to get it the way it should be!

*Are you sluggish, grumpy or do you have low libido?* Don't settle for it! That is not your best life. Get your hormones checked and find out what dietary changes you need to make. Enjoy every part of this life GOD has given you!

I know that there are still things left for me to do. My goal is to die young at an old age. Therefore, I am constantly seeking new ways to live longer. I encourage you to do the same. DO NOT DELAY. *Put this book down and DO IT NOW!*

## *Develop a Ritual*

A major corporation did a study on the impact of negative and disempowering words. *The study revealed that if you hear that you cannot do something once, you*

**must hear that you can do it seventeen times to neutralize the effects of that one negative statement!**

I believe negative words — through music, social media, TV, conversations, books, and all other mediums — have contributed greatly to the growing suicide rate. They say, "garbage in, garbage out." But I think that's wrong. I say, "garbage in, garbage stays!" The wrong environment can block your power, which is why you need to control your environment as much as possible. Some environmental exposures are out of your control but don't allow any negativity in your life that you can avoid. Your mind needs to be reprogrammed and you need to determine that *YOU* will be the one doing the programming!

If you don't program your mind, something or someone else will. You must train your mind to serve you, which is why you must develop a ritual to set the tone for greatness — to enrich you mentally, spiritually, and emotionally. Me personally, I take the time to get centered early when I first awaken. I listen to peaceful music and sounds that resonate with positive vibrations to my mind and body. You need to do some experimenting to find what works for you.

## *The Greatness Within to Win*

Keep in mind that for every negative word you hear, you need to hear seventeen positive words to neutralize that negativity. Therefore, your ritual should definitely include listening to positive, motivational messages and songs. If you need somewhere to start, go to YouTube and search for "Les Brown: Getting Unstuck," "It's Possible," and "Les Brown Speaking in the Georgia Dome." Millions of people all around the world listen to my voice every day and they say it has radically changed their lives.

People who were in dark places have found that something I've said inspired and empowered them to be HUNGRY enough to fight their way back to the light! Immerse yourself in a cycle of my messages and the messages of others who create positive, uplifting, and success-driven materials. Without the voices of powerful self-development giants such as Dr. Howard Thurman, Bishop T.D. Jakes, Zig Ziglar, Jim Rohn, Dr. Wayne Dyer, and others, I would not have made it this far. I kept them in my ear consistently.

I've spent thousands of hours developing myself with audiotapes, going to seminars and workshops, being a part of mastermind groups and reading two to three books per month. The average American only reads one book per year. If you commit to reading one book per month, in five years, you will have read sixty books, while most people will have only read five. That will make you an expert! Therefore, in addition to listening to messages, I encourage you to train yourself to read thirty to forty pages of something positive or educational, daily.

I have one last suggestion for your ritual. For many years, I kept a 3 x 5 index card that read on one side: "Ask and it shall be given you; seek, and you shall find; knock, and the door will be opened to you." The other side of the card read: "I give thanks that I am the world's greatest orator. I give thanks that I purchased my mother a home, fully furnished with everything paid for!"

I read these statements aloud daily and made vision boards that coincided with my goals. I reminded myself, by reading the card several times a day, what my goals were. I envisioned myself accomplishing those goals. I encourage you to do the same.

*How are you training your mind? What books are you reading? What messages are you listening to? What trainings are you attending?*

## *The Greatness Within to Win*

Commit to finding a minimum of ten resources that increase your knowledge capital and positively impact both your personal and professional life. Spend time every day sharpening your mind, developing yourself, upgrading your skills, and pursuing goals that are outside of your comfort zone. Decide to be self-dedicated. Work on yourself mentally, spiritually and emotionally. Operate in such a way that you **Grow Continuously**.

# *You've Got to be HUNGRY*

*Invest at least 10% of your income into your personal development because it is much more expensive to be ignorant than it is to invest in learning. The road to personal development never ends.*

**Chapter 6: Let go or Get dragged**

# Chapter Six

# Let Go or Get

# Dragged

## RELATionship IMPAct

### <u>Sometimes You Have to Do It Alone</u>

A friend of mine, by the name of Eula McClean, had a dream of moving from Alabama to Los Angeles to get into real estate. She saw what was happening in the real estate market and felt positive that she and her family could strike it rich in California. This was in the 1960s, during a time that many Black people had low expectations for their lives based on social injustice — but not Eula!

Eula was HUNGRY to go after her dream. Her goal was **Heart-Centered** and she had **Unshakable Faith** in her vision. She planned to earn money through childcare services and selling sweet potato pies by the slice. With the money she earned from those ventures, she would invest in a rental property and then repeat the process. At that time, Ms. Eula was married with two daughters, so she told her husband her ideas and asked him if the family would move and start this new life.

Her husband was hesitant to make the move and told her to take the kids and go without him. Mr. McClean insisted on staying behind in Alabama just in case things didn't work out and she needed to come back. He claimed he would move out West with her and the girls if things worked out as she planned. After some time, Eula exacted her vision and her real estate business was in profit. She and her daughters were living well.

Since all was going well, Eula asked her husband to come out and join them, as he said he would. However, he refused. She was devastated. She prayed to GOD to get her husband to see her vision and move to California to join the family. Eula told me that as she prayed, she heard a crystal- clear voice from GOD telling her, *"Do it alone."* She listened and let her husband stay where he was while she went on to amass over $300 million in real estate in Beverly Hills, CA. She lived in the same neighborhood as several celebrities, including Bob Hope!

Unfortunately, after some years passed, one of the McClean's daughters died. Finally, Mr. McClean, Eula's estranged husband, made it out West. He came only to attend his daughter's funeral. However, while there, he, at last, saw the lifestyle that his wife had created for herself and her family. He was undoubtedly amazed — probably ashamed and regretful too!

Eula told me that after the homegoing service ended, Mr. McClean asked her if she thought they could make it work between them again. At that request, Ms. Eula's jaw nearly hit the floor. She had no words for him and even accidentally laughed in his face! Needless to say, she sent him and his small mind back to his small life, in his small house, in his small town in Alabama while she continued to grow her big vision!

Sometimes the people who you expect to support you will indeed be the very ones who try to hinder your growth. Many times, the people who stand to benefit most from your success are the very ones you need to release. The people closest to you won't see your vision because it isn't theirs; they are often your number one fans in the discouragement club. That's okay! Be like Ms. Eula and do it alone! Pray to GOD to order your steps and take off!

There was a man who started a 400-million-dollar empire with a $500 loan from his mother. At some point, he hired his best friend to work alongside him. However, he eventually fired his friend. When asked why he did it, he responded flat-footedly, "If I didn't believe that I could be successful at what I was doing, I truly did not need someone on my payroll reminding me of that." HUNGRY people know that sometimes you must do it alone.

Sometimes even your closest friends and family must be cut from the team. Be ready to run on without them!

## *The Two Types of Relationships*

My son, John Leslie Brown, is a Professional Speaker and Consultant who coined a phrase that I love to use in my trainings. He asked the question, "Who can you count on and who should you count out?" Knowing who to *count out* is easy because there are only two types of relationships: nourishing relationships and toxic relationships. There is no room for in-between and no lukewarm or gray areas. People are either on your team and in support of you or they are not!

Nourishing relationships build you up. People who belong in this category recognize your potential. They see great things within you that you can't always see for yourself. Nourishing people aim to bring out the best in you. They sharpen your skills and learn from you. Toxic relationships, on the other hand, will drain you and can ultimately destroy you. People who fall into this category compromise your power and make you susceptible to many types of mental, emotional, and even physical disease.

There was a scientific study done that aimed to answer

the question: "What is it that determines the longevity of life?" I was sure the answer would be something like eating a plant-based diet or exercise or maybe prayer and meditation. I was wrong! The study found that **the NUMBER ONE determinant to a long life is having positive social interactions** — NOURISHING RELATIONSHIPS!

There is a term in psychiatry called "relationship illness." It speaks to the underlying toxic impact that relationships have on our lives — mentally, emotionally, and physically. Of people that are released from the hospital after a serious illness, the ones who go home to a social support system recover more quickly than the ones who go home to no one or to be alone. Most people are not mindful of the role that relationships play in living a positive, successful and adventurous life. They go to their graves early because their lives have been consumed by toxic, negative, draining emotional vampires.

*Are you in any relationships that aren't growing, relationships in which the other person is set in ways that are not progressive?*

Dr. Howard Thurman, mentor to Dr. Martin Luther King, Jr., and countless other religious leaders made a powerful statement that I aim to live by. He said that each of us should ask ourselves two very important questions in life.

The very first is, "Where am I going?" The second question is, "Who is going with me?"

Dr. Thurman said that if you ever ask those two questions in the wrong order, you will be in serious trouble!

I remember a lady who came to me to be mentored as a speaker. She wanted to do something that gave her a sense of meaning and purpose. I asked her, "Why do you want me to train you?"

Her response was, "Because you speak with your heart. I saw you captivate 80,000 people at the Georgia Dome!"

That was an acceptable answer, but as we continued to train together, I felt there was more that she had not told me — some unspoken reason that she wanted to transform people's lives. I asked her again, why she *really* wanted to be a speaker.

This time, she paused and, with tears in her eyes, said,

**"I've been a wife and I've been a mother, but I've never been *me*."** She went on to explain that for her to play those two roles, mother and wife, she thought she had to die to who she really was and who she could potentially become!

*You must ask yourself the question: "Who is holding me back from what I am working to become?"*

I believe that most people will never achieve their goals and dreams due to toxic relationships. In the same way, employers have performance assessments to determine who stays, goes, or gets promoted, you must perform assessments on your relationships. Everybody won't see your vision and not everyone can go with you to your next level. You've got to make those tough decisions based on their performance in your life. If you want to live a HUNGRY life, you must have the courage to look at each of your relationships and ask yourself.

*"Who am I becoming through my association with this person? Am I growing mentally, spiritually and financially through this relationship?"*

While pursuing my personal development and reaching for my destiny, I had to leave many relationships behind. This was most painful when I had to walk away from relationships that I thought would never end. But now, I truly believe the cliché that says, **"People come into your life for a reason, a season or a lifetime."** Don't make the mistake of thinking a *season* has to be long or even that the *reason* will have a positive impact on your growth. Like me, you must learn to let go of relationships that no longer help you grow or push you to greatness.

*I once saw a powerful quote. It read,* **"Don't waste time complaining about relationships that are sucking the life out of you when you're providing the straw."**

You might ask the question, "Les Brown, can't I help the people around me to change?" The answer is *NO! ABSOLUTELY NOT!* I remember trying to help my brother lose weight, but instead, I gained twenty-five pounds myself! *(laugh)* It's challenging enough working to transform your own self! You do not have the luxury of wasting time creating exercises and tests to attempt to change someone else. You should continue to believe for the day that your loved ones will become HUNGRY to live a different kind of life — a life of their own greatness. But until then, take the straw away and gift them with a copy of this book!

Leave unproductive people, places and things behind. "If you are always repairing potholes, you never have time to build new roads!" You are going to places that not everyone can go. Build the roads that lead to greatness that others can follow when they're ready, but don't let them slow you down. **Know who you can count on and who you must count out!**

## *Only Quality People*

Did you know that depressed people and their bad energy can rub off on you and impact your greatness? Just like placing a piece of rotten fruit in a basket can affect the rest of the fruit, people's negativity can cause our dreams to rot! The same way the common cold is spread through contact, so do common lives of mediocrity!

## *You've Got to be HUNGRY*

It's been said that you are the sum-total of the books you read and the five people with whom you most closely associate. I absolutely believe that we are the products of our environments. The people that we allow to have parts in our lives influence us on both a conscious level and subconscious level.

You may have heard the saying, "Your network determines your net worth." It is true! Statistics show that most people earn within three to five thousand dollars of their closest friends. The people you associate with have an impact on the well-being of every part of your life, from your health to your wealth. Dr. Dennis Kimbro says, "If you are the smartest person in your group, you need to get a new group." I would also add to that statement, if you are the biggest income earner in your group, you need two new groups. *(laugh!)*

As I always say, you must practice associating with **OQP** *(Only Quality People)*. These are the people who can take you places that you cannot go by yourself. You may have to change the people around you. One goose can fly 75 percent further in formation with other geese than it ever can flying solo. The same principle applies to you! You can run faster and further with one hundred people who want to go where you are going than you can with one hanging around your neck. But the truth is sometimes it can be hard to find nourishing relationships in your current environment. *Get into a new environment!* Take time to research clubs, groups, organizations and associations that share your interests and vision. Upgrade your circle! Ensure those around you match your HUNGER!

**Pause for a moment and ask yourself these two questions: What value is brought into my life by the people I interact with? What value do I bring to them?**

I remember the first time I had to speak to a massive crowd. The event was held at the Georgia Dome. I had been preparing for this day for quite some time and I felt ready to go on stage, take the mic and motivate the audience. I was fired up, inspired, and HUNGRY to speak. I felt sure of myself — *all the way up until the moment that I peeked out into the audience and saw 80,000 people!*

As soon as I saw the audience, my heart started beating so fast that I was convinced it would jump out of my chest! I felt as if I was about to faint and pee on myself. With every breath, I could literally feel all of my knowing slip away. It was like someone had flipped a switch and shut my brain down. Fear hijacked my mind and I felt nervous, terrified, and intimidated all at once!

I must have looked like everything I was thinking because my mentor, Mike Williams, came up to me, as I was pacing back and forth in the backstage area. He grabbed me by the shoulders and said, "Brownie, you can do this! Don't be intimidated by the crowd. You didn't come to see them; they are here to see you! You are Mamie Brown's boy! Make her proud!"

Mike had been my mentor for many years, ever since the fateful day that I called him from a payphone to tell him I was going to be a motivational speaker. There was something about the way in which he spoke that instantly calmed my fears. His words ignited a spirit of conviction and fearlessness in my heart that convinced me I could, indeed, inspire and motivate all 80,000 people in that stadium — including the event workers, the cleaning crew, and even parking lot attendants!

I remember a period when I suffered from panic attacks. I was speaking with one of my mentees, Dwight

Pledger, one day when anxiety set in. I was feeling very claustrophobic, as I thought about riding on an elevator. I told Dwight that I would take the stairs and meet him in the lobby. When I got downstairs, I was still feeling very unsettled.

Dwight came up to me and grabbed my hands and prayed with me and calmed me down. I noticed that some people recognized me. They probably thought he and I were a couple with the way we were standing. But I didn't care! His voice and his words were so peaceful that they immediately diffused my panic attack.

We will all have moments when we are not our best selves. That is why it is so critical to have people around you with high spiritual energy — people who can make a positive impact. The right people will always remind you that everything is alright. There is no way that we can predict what will happen to us in life, but it is GUARANTEED that there will come a time when we need someone to help us.

*Who can you count on? At the end of the day, Only Quality People will do!*

## *Let Go or Get Dragged!*

## *You've Got to be HUNGRY*

As you may guess, I get asked to speak at all types of events for all types of causes, themes, and audiences. I'm always surprised that, as someone who has been divorced three times, I still get asked to speak at couples' retreats. I guess people figure that I still have some wisdom to share concerning how to have healthy dating and marital relationships. And indeed, I do!

Getting divorced was an extremely tough decision each time. The last time was the most difficult. I was hurt, angry, and embarrassed. There I was telling people how to be successful and I couldn't make my own marriage work! I was, what some might call, "unlucky in love." Quite naturally, it took some time for me to let go of the baggage that I carried. However, I eventually found strength in a statement from Frankie Crocker:

***"It's better to be alone than to wish you were."***

I was once in a relationship where my growth was challenged daily. I had stopped being *Les Brown* to accommodate the other person's desires. Eventually, it began to impact my income and my performance. I looked in the mirror one day and said, "This is not me." I ended the relationship and — *BOOM!* To my surprise, everything changed! It was like a ton of weight had been lifted from my shoulders. In just one month, I generated over a half-million dollars. More than that, my peace and my joy came back and I again felt like myself.

A woman I know was in a toxic marriage. She noticed that she required some type of surgery every year she was married. After hearing one of my messages about toxic relationships, she filed for divorce. Would you believe that after finalizing her divorce, she was never again hospitalized or required any further surgery

### *Is your relationship making you sick?*

A study showed that a woman gains an average of fifty- five pounds in an unhealthy relationship. Many people gain unwanted weight in toxic relationships, they age prematurely, they are plagued with all types of illnesses, and they find themselves completely miserable. This is because most people never ask themselves:

**"What impact is this relationship having on me?"**

A friend of mine wrote a book called, *Women Who Carry Their Men*, after ending a relationship in which she was unequally yoked. She and her partner were *dying together*, as opposed to *living together*. She was growing and he wasn't. As she was reaching, he was settling. Ultimately, she realized that the relationship just couldn't work. My friend is not alone! Over fifty percent of married people are *dying together,* instead of *living together* because they have not stopped to ask the question: "Is this working for me?" It may be working for your partner, but is it working for YOU?

*Have you swallowed your voice? Have you gone along for the ride and become someone that you don't know? Has the dichotomy between your public success and the private failure in your relationship become unbearable?*

You owe it to yourself to summon the courage and faith to face the truth that your life isn't working! The person you are with has become someone you cannot have peace with. You are about to lose your mind! You've got to be free — *they've got to go!* Going along just to get along no longer works for you. Let go of relationships that are no longer befitting or they will drag you down! *Let go or get dragged!*

So many people rush to be in a relationship with someone else when their relationship with themselves is either non-existent or detrimental to their success! A lot of people practice self-sabotaging behaviors; these are toxic behaviors, which manifest to an even greater degree in relationships. Spending the time to get to know yourself and what your needs are is essential.

There are certain personal development milestones you should reach **before** you attempt to become one with another, in a "significant other" type of relationship. I've found that often people will choose a mate and then suffer from, what I call, *delayed enlightenment*. This happens, when somewhere down the road, you discover that the person you're with isn't who you thought they were, and they discover the same thing about you. I believe this phenomenon of *delayed enlightenment* contributes to the high divorce rate. However, it is inevitable that this will happen, when people choose a partner without truly getting to learn themselves first!

One of my most painful experiences was when I found out that my best friend, Bou, had been in his house suffering and alone for at least a week. I had unsuccessfully been trying to reach him for several days. When I finally went out to his house to check on him, he was in bad shape. I was heartbroken and took him back to my home in Potomac, Maryland. Bou's wife was a flight attendant and was gone most of the time. While he was with me, she never even called to ask where he was or to let me know that she thought he may have been missing.

I have found that we often overlook small and seemingly insignificant toxic traits in a person because we want to see the best in our friends and loved ones — this includes significant others! We often stop assessing marriage relationships because we are adamant that marriage means *forever*. Of course, no one gets married with divorce in mind. But we don't get married with neglect, loneliness, losing touch without ourselves, or misery in mind either!

There will be occasional conflict in any relationship. However, if both parties cannot resolve problems respectfully and with ease, that may be a sign that the relationship has reached its endpoint. If the relationship is not thriving and has stopped growing, it is probably dying. Anything stagnant eventually becomes putrid! Even a relationship that starts off positive, may unfortunately then go south. You must be willing to continuously monitor your relationships — yes, your marriage too.

*Always ask yourself, "Is this working for me?"*

## <u>*Don't Be That Guy!*</u>

*We've discovered that there are two types of people in relationships — people you can count on and people you must count-out. But have you ever stopped to ask yourself, "Which type of person am I being?*

Often in life, people are expecting to receive what they are not willing to give. The key to cultivating nourishing relationships is to first nourish your relationship with GOD and then your relationship with yourself. You cannot nourish an external relationship when your intrinsic relationship with self is malnourished! How can you feed someone's soul when you have no soul food to offer?

I remember how happy I was when I really started to make a significant income as a speaker. I came home one weekend with over $100,000 in cash. When I arrived home, I was bearing gifts for my son, John Leslie. I called him into the room and I gave him all the gifts I'd bought him. I then showed him the money that I'd earned. I laid the money out on the bed and had him help me count it!

My son was fourteen at the time. I had placed six

figures worth of cash in his hands. I was so proud of myself and grateful for the life I was giving him. I had this invincible feeling. I thought back to the leftover food I ate and the hand-me-down clothes I wore when I was a child. At that moment counting cash with my son, I had the assurance that he would never experience that. I thought to myself, *"I have done it; I have WON!"*

Not long afterward, John Leslie came back into the room and handed me a handwritten note that read:

**"Daddy I am so proud of you. You're doing a good job. Thank you for the presents, but what I want is your presence."**

Looking back over my life and career, I realize that my HUNGER for greatness did not include a focus on being a great father and husband. I was HUNGRY to provide financially and materially, but I fell short in providing emotionally. I fell short in providing my presence — simply being *there* and being *available*.

It takes more than money and material things to nourish a relationship. There is nothing more valuable than time. If I had my life to live over again, I'd make sure that my magnificent obsession included having healthy, flourishing relationships with my loved ones. I would learn how to say 'no' to things much earlier in life, spend more time at home, and cherish the presence of my family much more than I did. I implore you not to make this mistake.

> *What value do you bring to your relationships?*
> *How much time are you investing in them?*

I have made this point clear: *Don't be in a toxic relationship.* Let me make this point even clearer: **Don't be the toxic person in a relationship!** Don't allow someone to suck the life out of you, but *don't suck the life out of someone else* either. In our society, we are so quick to "cut people off," but sometimes the relationship is not working because of YOU. Have you ever stopped to consider that YOU might be the problem? Don't be that guy! Don't be that girl!

*I challenge you to take inventory of your relationships. Evaluate them carefully. Inspect the value others bring to you and the value you bring to others. Do you need to step up your game?*

You can never afford to look past the importance of healthy relationships. Just like Mike Williams gave me the right words at the right time for me to go on the stage at the Georgia Dome — and not potentially damage my career as a speaker — someone can give you the wrong words at an inopportune time, causing a disaster in your life! But you must realize that you can have that same impact on others. You're either speaking right words or wrong words. You are for them or you are against them!

### WHO ARE YOU IN YOUR RELATIONSHIPS

### -The "Count On" or the "Count Out" Person?

I mentioned earlier how Sam Axelrod showed a special interest in me. The fact is, there were other guys on the sales team, but I was the only one who paid attention to Sam's wisdom. Sam loved to teach, but a teacher that has no student has no purpose. I met a need in Sam's life by allowing him to pour into me.

There is a saying that goes, "When the student is ready, the teacher shows up." You could also reverse that and say, "When the teacher is ready, the student shows up!" Sam could count on me to show up, ready to learn each day and that brought value to his life as well as mine.

## The Greatness Within to Win

HUNGRY people understand that right relationships are essential. HUNGRY people understand what value they bring to a relationship. Relationships matter and the part you play in a relationship matters. One of the keys to living your greatest life is to surround yourself with positive, collaborative, achievement-driven relationships. As the great Eryka Badu says; "Pick your relationships like you pick your fruit". It's okay to be selective or even choosy because your relationships will always have some impact on your future... hopefully for the better.

# You've Got to be HUNGRY

*Always take a step back and ask yourself: If I surrounded myself with people like myself would I become the next greatest version of myself?*

BE THE QUALITY PERSON OTHERS CAN COUNT ON!

## Chapter 7: "Drink Rock, Drink"

# Chapter Seven

# "Drink Rock, Drink!"

## YES LORD

## *What's the Hold Up?*

For over fourteen years, I attended seminars and workshops to watch great motivational speakers. There was something in my heart that kept saying, *"This is you!"* But there was something else in my mind that was saying, *"You can't do that, Les Brown. You don't have a degree. You have never worked for a major corporation. You can't compete with people who have the qualifications you don't have!"*

HUNGER is a calling that you must answer with a humble and faith-filled *YES!* There is a song called *Yes* by Shekinah Glory. I will never forget the impact it had on me when I first heard it. I thought about the many years that I'd run from this calling to be a motivational speaker. When I think of the courage that it took for my mother to adopt seven children, when I think of the repeated risks that she took to answer the call on her life — it makes me wonder what took me so long! Mamie Brown was an exemplary model of what it means to yield and say, **"YES LORD."**

Even though we were poor, we didn't know it. Mama's love, care, and protection sheltered us, as much as possible, from the harsh realities of life. I remember a rough period when Mama wasn't physically able to work. We were low on food. My little sister, Margaret Ann, who was four at the time, tried to open a can of sardines. When she failed to completely open the can, she left it out on the counter.

When Mama discovered the partially opened can of sardines, she realized that they might have spoiled. Not wanting to waste a meal, but also knowing that we could possibly get ill from eating the sardines, she told us to go outside so she could eat some first and see if she became sick. However, I refused to leave Mama's side, and instead, wait with her. Fortunately, she did not get sick. We were able to share the few sardines that we had available and not miss a meal!

Mama was always my hero. She saved my life and the lives of my brothers and sisters, multiple times — simply because she embraced her destiny. Because it was her calling, she did whatever she had to do, however, she had to do it, to keep us safe. There is another incident that sticks out in my mind as I reflect on my mother's commitment to her calling.

One day, Mama and I were out shopping on a very hot

day in downtown Miami. It was probably in the high nineties and I was very thirsty. Like a mirage in the desert, I saw a water fountain alongside the path we were walking. Before she knew what was happening, I let go of Mama's hand and ran to the fountain. I quickly climbed up the step and began taking large, satisfying gulps of water. However, my satisfaction was short-lived.

Out of nowhere, Mama came up to me and snatched me away from the fountain. She started violently punching and beating me in the head and face. She had a crazed look in her eyes, as she beat me. She was screaming, "Don't you ever do that again! DON'T YOU EVER DO THAT AGAIN!!!"

I was shocked and scared. I started screaming back, "Mama, it's me! Mama, please it's me! It's ME!"

After a while, a White police officer came over with a sneer on his face. He had his billy club in his right hand and he was pounding it into the palm of his left hand. It made a terrifying smacking sound, as it landed on his palm. Then, with an intimidating glare, he spoke. "Alright, that's enough, girl. You've beat that little nigger boy enough. Now, I won't have to beat him." He then walked away with a wicked laugh.

I was crying, confused, humiliated and half dazed. Mama was sobbing profusely, as she began to comfort me by hugging me tightly. She cradled my little tear-stained and bruised face in her hands as she kissed it repeatedly. She looked at me with teary and remorseful eyes. "I'm sorry, Leslie, I'm so sorry. Please forgive me."

"Mama, why did you beat me like that?" I could barely get the words out through my deep, gasping sobs.

"Leslie, that water fountain was for Whites only. We can't drink from that kind of fountain — ever!"

"Why, Mama?"

"That's just the way it is, Leslie. I hit you like that so the policeman wouldn't. Because if he had hit you with that Billy Club, I would have fought him until he killed me! Then I would have left you and your brothers and sisters to fend for yourselves." Mama was still weeping as she explained how she had just saved both of our lives by beating me.

That was a life-changing moment for me at five years old. I realized that there were certain things I could not do and certain places I could not go because of the color of my skin. But in retrospect, I realize that these experiences contributed greatly to the HUNGER that people often ask me about. My drive and HUNGER were developed at a very young age watching how hard my mother worked to single-handedly raise seven children that she didn't give birth to. She understood her calling and she always said *'YES.'*

Can you imagine having to beat your precious, five-year-old child like a maniac just to save his life and yours? You'd think that would be a difficult decision to make, but Mama didn't even have to *think*. That cop was eyeing me from the moment I approached the fountain. He had in mind to do me harm and Mama had to create a strong distraction! She *knew* what it would take to be true to the calling on her life and — at that moment, in an instant — she simply said *'YES!'*

How could she claim to be taking good care of me if she allowed me to be beaten by a grown man with a Billy Club? How could she take good care of me and my twin brother and ensure that we were never separated if she positioned herself to get killed? Therefore, it was not a hard decision at all. She simply said *'YES'* to her calling. I shudder to think what could have become of me and my siblings had my mother not said *'YES'* to her calling. What if she decided to wait for fourteen years as I did? I may not be the *Les Brown* today!

**Have you ever thought about something that you want to do and then allowed your logic, practicality and reasoning to talk you right out of it? What's really the holdup?**

I mean after all, you're just being "realistic," right? There is an African proverb that goes, "If there is no enemy within, the enemy without can do us no harm." Shakespeare said, "The fault, dear Brutus, is not in our stars but in ourselves." For fourteen years, I said 'no' to the calling on my life. For fourteen years, I could have been motivating and inspiring people around the globe. I could have been saving lives and motivating our youth. But because of my own logic, and judging myself according to how I appeared, I said *'no'* to my destiny. A gentleman by the name of Robert Roots said, "It's not what you don't have; it's what you think you need, that stops you from being happy and successful." All that I really needed was to believe and simply say, *'YES' — just like Mama.*

It wasn't until I answered GOD's calling on my life that

I was able to experience the fullness of the possibilities that awaited me. The future that is unfolding for you can only look as bright as your willingness to accept your purpose, your willingness to accept your calling. *You've Got to Say, 'YES!'*

## Hello Mr. Butterball. My Name Is...

When I travel to speak, people will inevitably request that I tell the story of how I became a disc jockey in Miami. It seems they never tire of hearing this story and, honestly, I never get tired of telling it *(smile!)* The whole thing started when a high school teacher named Mr. Leroy Washington recognized something great in me. Mr. Washington believing in me, and pushing me in the right direction, led me to begin the career which would catapult me into becoming the man I am today.

I often celebrate Mr. Washington for his role in my life. It meant the world to me then and still does today. Throughout high school, Mr. Washington would let me come to his house and spend time with him and his family. After I graduated, Mr. Washington helped me get a scholarship so I could enter Florida A & M University. I was very nervous and unsure about going to college, which is why I got a job as a backup — working as a garbage collector for the Miami Sanitation Department.

However, despite my uncertainty, I was excited about the possibility of going to college. That excitement all but left once I spoke to the guidance counselor of the school. During our conversation, she said, "Leslie, you know you are not college material and Mr. Washington will not be at FAMU to help you. Give this opportunity to someone more deserving. I beg you, don't embarrass yourself. Most importantly, don't embarrass Mr. Washington because you know you will fail, don't you?"

I reluctantly agreed and said, "Yes, I know."

She went on to say, "Now, you have a decent job making ten dollars an hour. You'll be fine. You're going to have a good career there at the Sanitation Department."

I gave up on the idea of going to college and embraced my life as a garbage collector. My first pickup was the garbage that came from that guidance counselor's mouth! Not having a college education haunted me for many years and was often the reason that I was too insecure to take advantage of opportunities. It was the biggest contributing factor for me hesitating for over fourteen years. Don't ever let someone's opinion of you define how you see yourself and what you're capable of!

200

# The Greatness Within to Win

### You've Got to Be HUNGRY!

Of course, as fate would have it, one day while I was working on my route, we came across Mr. Washington's street. I prayed so hard that he wouldn't be at home because I had been avoiding his calls. He knew I had never started college and he had been trying to contact me. My prayer request was quickly denied. As we rode down his street, not only was he home, he was standing right outside on his porch! It was as if his spirit told him to just find *anything* to throw away right at the moment we pulled up in front of his house. I quickly grabbed a big garbage can and lifted it up on my right side in an attempt to prevent Mr. Washington from seeing me.

As it turned out, neither I nor that big garbage can was invisible or inconspicuous and I heard Mr. Washington's booming voice say, "Mr. Brown!"

I kept walking away with the garbage can. The other guys in the truck said, "Hey man, that guy's calling you!"

He called for me again. "Les Brown!"

I emptied the trash and turned around. "Yes, sir."

He walked down off his porch and told me to come in for a minute for a brief talk.

"Oh, Mr. Washington, look at me. I'm dirty and have this stinking garbage all over me. I'll come back this weekend."

As I turned to leave, Mr. Washington shouted to the crew, "Hey, would you guys like to have some ice water?"

I quickly tried to volunteer an answer on behalf of the crew. "Oh no, sir. We're busy. We have a lot of work to do."

Much to my dismay, the truck driver didn't agree. He said. "Come on man! We've got some time. We'll take a break."

We all went on the porch and Ms. Washington brought us some water. I was beyond embarrassed and waiting dreadfully for the question that I knew was coming.

While the other crew members got to enjoy their moment of reprieve, Mr. Washington approached me privately. "What happened to you? I've been calling you and you haven't returned any of my calls. Your mother told me she gave you my messages. I got word that you're not going to take advantage of the scholarship that I secured for you."

I told him about my meeting with the counselor.

Mr. Washington locked eyes with me intently and

asked, "Les Brown, Do YOU believe that you would have succeeded had you had gone to college?"

"To be honest with you, Sir, no."

"Mr. Brown, I know that hitting the books is a struggle for you and it takes you longer to learn things than most people. But I also know that you are a young man who will work hard once you're into something and give it everything you have."

Amid this brief dialogue, the guys finished their water and were ready to get back to work. The driver shouted out, "Okay, let's go!" and I gladly headed out with them.

As we drove off, Mr. Washington stood on his porch staring at me and shaking his head.

I must've felt Mr. Washington's conviction because I quit my job as a garbage collector very soon after that day. Since Mr. Washington didn't live too far from me, I would go by and visit him, from time to time. One day while visiting, he asked me what it was that I really wanted to do. I told him that I was interested in becoming a disc jockey.

"Well, here's what I want you to do." He gave me his car keys and said, "At noon, I want you to go out and get into my car and turn on the radio. There's a guy named

Paul Harvey, who does a program called *The Rest of the Story*. He's the greatest personality on radio. If you want to be good at something, Mr. Brown, you must study the people who have mastered it."

As we continued to talk, he told me to start listening to Paul Harvey regularly and to develop my communication skills. He ended by saying, "Once you open your mouth, you tell the world who you are."

After a period of listening to the show that Mr. Washington had suggested and other radio personalities, I started to develop my own style. I was mimicking the greatest DJs of that time. Once I felt confident enough, I asked Mr. Washington to listen to my audition. I performed as if I was an on-air personality and then asked him, "What do you think?"

Mr. Washington was delighted to hear my pitch. "It's pretty good, Mr. Brown!" He gave me the keys to his car again. But this time, he told me to drive to WMBM radio station on Miami Beach. He told me once I got there, I should ask for the program director, Milton "Butterball" Smith. He instructed me, "Tell Mr. Butterball, I sent you!"

I was fired up! I went to the station and when the program director came out, I greeted him. "Hello Mr.

Butterball. I was sent here by Mr. Washington. My name is Les Brown and I'd like to be a disc jockey, sir."

He looked at me with a puzzled expression. "Do you have any broadcasting or journalism in your background?"

"No, sir, I don't. But please let me audition for you, sir. I've imagined myself being on the air, practiced, and listened to a lot of radio. I'm sure I will be very good."

He looked me up and down. "No, I don't have any job for you."

I left and went back to Mr. Washington and told him what happened. Mr. Washington was unmoved saying, "Don't take it personally, Leslie. Most people are so negative, they will have to say 'no' seven times before they say 'yes'. Go back and try again."

So, the next day, I went back again. I walked into the station with a smile. "How are you, Mr. Butterball? My name is Les Brown, sir."

"What do you want?" He was unenthusiastic, to say the least.

"I'd like to become a disc jockey, sir."

"Weren't you here yesterday?" he
retorted. "Yes, sir."

"Didn't I tell you 'no yesterday?"

"Yes, sir."

"Then why are you back today?"

Undeterred, I answered him, "Well, sir, I didn't know whether or not someone was fired or laid off."

Mr. Butterball was not amused. "No one was laid off and no one was fired. Now get on out of here."

Remembering that Mr. Butterball might say 'no' seven times, I took Mr. Washington's advice and went back again. I didn't care about the *'no'*; I wasn't afraid of the rejection. I knew I was more than capable. I was confident that I would make a successful disc jockey and I was **HUNGRY** to make it happen! On the third day, I returned talking loudly and looking happy, as if I were seeing the station manager for the first time. "Hello, Mr. Butterball. How are you? My name is Les Brown, sir, and I'd like to be a disc jockey."

"I know what your name is. Weren't you in here the last two days?" At this point, Mr. Butterball was extremely annoyed.

"Yes, sir."

"And didn't I tell you 'no' the last two days?" "Yes, sir."

With anger in his voice, he spoke through gritted teeth, "So why are you back again today?"

"Well, sir. I didn't know whether or not someone had gotten sick or died, sir."

"No one has gotten sick or died. No one was laid off or fired. Now, don't you come back here again!!"

Mr. Butterball shouted with a tone that clearly stated 'period, end of story!' Nonetheless, as you can well imagine, I got up the next morning, got dressed and went back for the fourth day. I had a smile on my face, looking happy and talking loudly, "Hello Mr. Butterball. How are you? My name is Les Bro—"

But this time, before I could even finish my sentence, Mr. Butterball interrupted me. "Go get me some coffee!" I eagerly replied. "Yes, sir!"

As I've mentioned many times in my messages, every 'no' gets you closer to a 'YES!' Because of my perseverance, Mr. Butterball allowed me to hang around the radio station. I would run errands for the DJs — errands such as getting coffee, lunch or dinner for them. I would go to the control rooms to take the DJs their food. While in there, I'd take advantage of the opportunity to stand against the wall and watch them work the controls. I just knew my time would come, so I kept visualizing myself on the air.

After a few months rolled by, one glorious Sunday afternoon, my time finally came! I was at the radio station with a disc jockey named Rocking Roger. Rock was drinking while on air. I was the only one there with him. As I looked at him through the control room window, my wheels started turning because I could feel what was coming next. I was pacing back and forth, watching him, as if on the prowl — *because I was young, I was ready, and I was HUNGRY!*

Rock was in bad shape and it was getting worse by the minute, but I said, "Drink, Rock, drink!" I would have even gotten him some more if he'd asked me to! *(laugh)*

Eventually, Rock got so drunk that he could not complete his show. The phone rang and I answered. It was the general manager announcing himself. "This is Mr. Kline."

"I know, Mr. Kline," I said.

"Rock can't finish the show," Mr. Kline stated in distress.

"I know." I was working hard to hide my excitement!

"I need you to call in one of the other DJs. Can you do that?"

I told him that *I could,* but it didn't mean that *I would!* After hanging up, I said to myself, "Now, this man must think I'm crazy!" I had no intention of calling another DJ when the best DJ in the nation was already in the building! The only people I called were Mama and my girlfriend, Cassandra. I told them, "Y'all turn up the radio, come out on the front porch and listen. I'm 'bout to come on the air!"

I waited for about twenty minutes and then called Mr. Kline back. "Mr. Kline, I can't find anybody to come in on the weekend, sir."

"Young boy, do you know how to work the controls?"

I had been studying those controls for months, waiting for that very moment; I was ready! "I sure do, sir."

What Mr. Kline said next were the words that I had been waiting to hear — the words that my HUNGER always knew would one day be spoken: "Go in there and work the controls, but you don't say nothing. You hear?"

I didn't care about anything he said past: *"Go in there and work the controls..."* I eagerly agreed! I was so excited that I was tingling all over. I walked into that control room with total confidence that the world was about to experience the manifestation of the best-kept secret in the history of radio! It was time for my long-awaited and highly anticipated debut!

I put on a fast record by Little Stevie Wonder, a record called *Fingertips.* I then sat down behind the turntables, opened my mouth and said: "Lookout! This is me, LB, Triple P, Les Brown, your Platinum Playing Papa! There were none before me and there will be none after me, therefore, that makes me the one and only! Young and single and love to mingle — certified, bona fide and indubitably qualified to bring you satisfaction and a whole lot of action. Look out baby, I'm your Love Man!"

*I was HUNGRY for a 'YES' and didn't stop until I got one!*

After hearing me DJ, it was undeniable to Mr. Butterball that I'd be more of an asset to the radio station as a disc jockey than an errand boy. I was hired as a part-time DJ on the weekends and eventually given my own show! I was unstoppable! *You've Got to Be HUNGRY!*

## <u>*Just Say 'YES'*</u>

No matter how old you may be, I strongly believe that

until you discover why you are living, you've never lived at all! I am convinced that all of us were created **on purpose, for a purpose, and with a purpose.** Just as there is a calling on my life, there is a calling on your life. The Creator created us to create. For this reason, each of us has a special mark placed upon our lives — something that only the person who carries it can deliver to The Universe. There's but one requirement — you must say *'YES'* to the HUNGER that is in your heart.

For a long time, I was sitting on the bench of life operating out of a small mindset. I wanted more, but I didn't believe in myself. I wasn't HUNGRY and I didn't know the truth about who I really am. I knew I enjoyed making people laugh and feel good about themselves, but I couldn't see the bigger picture. Even though the signs were there, I kept saying:

*"No, not me. I don't have a college education."*
*"No, not me. I was labeled educable mentally retarded."*
*"No, not me. I failed twice in school."*
*"No, not me. I'm not wealthy; I'm not even rich." "No, not me. I don't know the right*

*people." "No, not me. I have the complexion of rejection." "No, No, NO... NOT ME!"*

My internal dialogue was entirely negative. I was so busy responding to my negative, *counter-calling* that I couldn't even hear the question I was being asked. GOD was asking me if I was ready to move — ready to change myself, my situation, and my people. But I kept saying, *"No, not me!"* For years I was suffering while accepting a self-imposed life of mediocrity. I was *living a misplaced life* because I did not dare to simply say, "**YES, LORD.**"

Studies indicate that over eighty percent of our self-talk is negative. I remember having the opportunity to be in a play. I auditioned and earned the starring role. I was both excited and petrified, at the same time. The director believed that I could do it, but I didn't believe that I could do it. I was so afraid that I decided not to show up for rehearsals. I was eventually replaced. My negative self-talk talked me right out of an opportunity that I was qualified to fulfill!

I will never forget the shame I felt as I debated with myself over whether I should attend the play. Begrudgingly, I decided to go. Still feeling embarrassed, I wore a hat and shades, so as not to be recognized. I sat all the way in the back, in the dark, and I cried as I watched the other person play the role that I had not permitted myself to accept. I felt that it should have been me on that stage. It would have been me on that stage if I hadn't given into fear — *if I'd only said, 'YES'.*

I can't tell you the number of times that I passed up opportunities to do meaningful things. I felt inferior to others on so many occasions, particularly when it came to people who I perceived as having more education than me. Because I didn't have a college degree, I consciously decided to say 'no' in all kinds of situations. I clearly had the ability to effectively perform. Other people saw it in me, but I did not see it in myself — and so I said '*NO.*'

What I needed at that point in my life was to say '*YES!*' '*YES*' to my dream. '*YES*' to my life. '*YES*' to my potential. '*YES*' to the opportunities that were presented to me. But instead, I just kept saying 'no'. However, there came a time when I could no longer run from my destiny or ignore the signs. There came a time when I was forced to get still and hear the calling on my life. It was then that I finally had the life-defining moment of saying, "**YES, LORD**. I hear You and I will follow You."

They say, "Better late than never." Sure, that has a ring of truth. But I say, "Better NOW than later!" I suppressed my own victory for so long. We can all escape our greatness if we choose to, but I promise you, none of us were designed for mediocrity. Living in the negative of self- rejection produces such an ugly, stripped-down life. There is peace when we live in the affirmative. There is freedom in our *YES*; there is beauty in our *YES*.

Nonetheless, studies indicate that eighty-six percent of people say 'no' to their dreams because of their fears — the fear of losing, the fear of being rejected, the fear of failure. Be a part of the other fourteen percent! No matter what your dreams are, don't you dare ask yourself the question: "How am I ever going to do this?" The "how" is really none of your business because, the truth is, it is not you who is going to make it happen anyway! Instead of asking the fear-driven question of "how", take the position of commitment. The position of commitment is this: You do what you already know how to do and don't worry about what you don't know how to do!

***Do what you can and let GOD do what you can't!*** *It is He Who has called you and He will NOT let you fail* *when you've done all you can!!! But **You've Got to Be***

***HUNGRY** enough to simply say, "**YES, LORD!**"*

It will not be easy! Before you achieve your greatness, I strongly believe that you are going to go through some very difficult challenges. I like to call them "character-building opportunities" and there will be plenty of them. There will be sacrifices to be paid, a lot of pain and surprising setbacks and disappointments that you must endure. The distance between who you are now and where you want to go may be so wide that you can't even fathom the end. But as I always say, "When life knocks you down, try and land on your back because if you can look up, you can get up!"

If you are like I used to be — sitting on the sidelines of life for fourteen years suffering from possibility blindness — my wish for you is that you say 'YES', to your dreams, *RIGHT NOW!* Saying "**YES, LORD**" was the best thing that could have happened to me. It was at that moment that I realized that I had done the first part of my life *my way* and gotten subpar results. When I finally said 'YES', I made the decision that I would do it *GOD's way* for the remainder and get supernatural results! I am fortunate to be in my seventies and still here to say, "**YES, LORD!**"

## *You've Got to be HUNGRY*

Say *'YES'* to a better future. Say *'YES'* to a new opportunity and the next greatest version of you! Say *'YES'* despite adversities, daunting odds, and previous failures. Even when people desert you and no longer believe in you and work against you, say *'YES!'* Even when you've been ripped off, say *'YES!'* Even when you've made a lot of stupid mistakes say *'YES!'* Say *'YES' from* the bottom of your heart and soul and spirit. Say *YES!* Say to yourself, *"This is mine; victory is mine."* Everything may be telling you to turn around and go back. Don't listen! Still say *"YES, and move forward now!"*

*Give yourself the experience of living in the affirmative! Say 'YES' to a better life. Give life a chance to prove to you that you truly are a masterpiece because you are a piece of The Master!*

**Chapter 8: The Story Never Told**

# Chapter Eight

# The Story Never Told

# HUNGER Tested & Tried

I've been sharing messages on the importance of HUNGER for fifty years. I've shared many stories of *failing my way to success* and being tested. But nothing in my life has tested my HUNGER — *my sheer will to live* — like what I am about to share with you next.

If anyone has ever doubted whether what I teach works, you will not doubt after reading this. **Without HUNGER**, *I would not have survived to tell this story...*

## *How It All Began*

One of my mentees, Dwight Pledger, shared something with me that I've reflected on for a while. He said, "We all lead three distinct lives: our public lives, our private lives, and our secret lives." The conversation we were having reminded me of an out of print book, *"Why Am I Afraid to Tell You Who I Am... because You may not like it and it's all I've got!"*

Secrets are the things that we keep hidden away from the world because we are afraid of how the public and private layers of our lives will be impacted. Sometimes no one else knows our secrets while other secrets are shared. Because secrets are usually hidden within a person, you could spend nearly every waking moment with someone or talk to them every day and still never know certain things about them!

However, I think the worst secrets are the ones that we keep from ourselves. Often, our secret lives stem from deep-seated denial about weaknesses and issues we find too challenging to face. I have always prided myself on being a shoot-from-the-hip, transparent type of person. However, after reflecting on the book mentioned and my mentee's quote, I realized that for me to fully represent all that I speak about, I needed to stop living a "secret life."

It took deep introspection and self-reflection and a lot of courage, to be honest with myself and admit that for several years I, Les Brown — famous motivational speaker, source of inspiration to many and someone who has vehemently fought against drug abuse — *was addicted to prescription pain killers.*

When the cancer I'd been dealing with for twenty-seven years came back with a vengeance and spread throughout my body, I was racked with pain every day. To make it worse, it was more than just the cancer pain and the accompanying stress that made my body ache. I was facing several health challenges, including diabetes, heart issues and sciatica pain. *(Sciatica causes a shooting pain to radiate from the back, down the sciatic nerve in the legs).* In short, the pain that I was going through was excruciating!

Despite my varied conditions, I was still working hard to make a global impact, determined to be unstoppable. I was moving relentlessly and had a nonstop schedule, packed with speaking engagements and training seminars. I was resolute about beating my health conditions and rising above my circumstances! However, it seemed the more I traveled, the more pain I experienced. It was hard to accept that there were certain things that I could not do in my condition and I pushed myself to dangerous limits.

I remember the day that sciatica pain made a proper introduction of itself. I was at the airport going through security. I bent over to pick up my carry-on to place it on the conveyor belt. When I bent over, I felt a painful lump on my spine. I had never felt that before, so it shocked me. I remained bent over for several moments, trying to gather myself and then made the regretful decision to just "muscle through it." As I attempted to stand up, with my suitcase in hand, I felt the most intense pain that I'd ever known in my life. I let out a gut-wrenching scream that echoed throughout the entire airport and then collapsed to the ground, writhing in pain.

I am not sure what hurt most at that point — the physical pain or the emotional agony of the embarrassment I was feeling, as security rushed over to help me up and place me in a wheelchair! That is when sciatica spoke to me, as if it were the bad guy in a movie, letting the good guy hero know that he had met his match: "You better recognize who I am! Because I will NOT BE IGNORED!"

From that day forward, my health issues continued to plague me in a very real way. There was no level of muscling through it or mind over matter that successfully conquered the pain that seemed to be constantly conquering me. I was forced to respect its power and at various points, it was so severe that I had to deliver my messages from stage in a wheelchair. My physical deterioration and the fact that I could not hide it was very mentally and emotionally challenging.

My desire to stay on task with my demanding schedule

and still monitor my health had me seeing multiple doctors for multiple conditions who prescribed multiple medications. With all these different doctors, none who were in communication with the other, I was prescribed several powerful painkillers. The doctors had me convinced that for me to heal and keep my pain at bay enough to function, I had to follow this intense medical protocol. I trusted their medical advice, so I didn't challenge any of it. I popped every pill that each of them prescribed and just went about my business from day-to-day.

One day, I was watching the news and a report came on which discussed the growing prescription opioid crisis in the

U.S. I listened in surprise, but it didn't register to me that *I was included in this epidemic.* As fate would have it, several days later, I heard a public service announcement on the radio advertising-free resources for people who were taking addictive medications such as hydrocodone, codeine, oxycodone, morphine, fentanyl, and others.

I was taking every drug listed in the ad. I remember thinking to myself, *"I'm taking all those drugs and I'm not addicted. I wonder what's wrong with the people who are!"* As I said, the worst secrets are the ones we keep from ourselves!


## *The Intervention*

Because this regimen went on for several years, I can't really say exactly when I became addicted. However, considering the mere fact that the drugs are designed to be addictive, it stands to reason that I was probably hooked on the pain pills shortly after starting them and for quite a while. Within a few months of the PSA test results that revealed the cancer had come back, the number of pills I was being prescribed had increased significantly. It reached a point that I was taking a combination of pills, three times each day, up to seventy-five pills per day! I had no quality of life. I had become a slave to my pill-taking regimen and my work schedule.

Even though *my* eyes were closed to the dilemma I was in, my children's eyes were wide open. They were watching me closely and had become very concerned. They passed their concerns on to me in hopes that I would realize that I needed to make some serious adjustments to my pain management regimen. I let my children know that I appreciated their concern for me.

However, I had been told by my doctors that this life was going to be my "new normal." My children were the ones who were right, though. I should have listened to them!

I started having lapses of memory, which made it nearly impossible for me to travel alone or even drive around town. I had strangers come up to me and ask if I was okay. Random people came to my aid, on more than one occasion, and I would have no memory of what had taken place that required their assistance. I was up talking and working all night. I was irritated often. My behavior and moods were completely altered and I wasn't sleeping. I could barely function and I didn't feel like myself at all.

I still don't remember the nine-day hospital stay that my children described to me. My only recollection is leaving with my son, Patrick, who is the one that came to pick me up when I was discharged. Despite what he was telling me, I did not believe that I could have been in a hospital bed that long! I refused to believe him until he showed me pictures of me and my kids in the hospital on various days. The proof was in the pictures; I was in shock and extremely emotional.

When we got in the car to leave, Patrick told me that

he would be driving me to my daughter Serena's house. I felt relieved to be going there because I could rest, share some quality time with my daughter and her family — and of course, *get back to work!* Much to my surprise, when we arrived at Serena's, there were cars parked everywhere. Obviously, rest was not on the agenda, so I asked Patrick if there was a party going on inside. "Just come in. You'll see," he said.

When I walked in, my children and my mentor, Mike Williams, were in the living room along with a couple that I didn't recognize. My gut instinct told me exactly what was going on. This was no party; this is an intervention. Back in my earlier days I had been referred to as the "Intervention King"; I know an intervention when I see one! I thought it a little odd that I'd be brought to an intervention straight from the hospital. But, then again, not really. Everyone knows that I'm always ready to help!

The room was tense and silent. Everyone was looking at me and I was looking at them. I was the one who finally broke the silence. "Hey, is this an intervention for someone?"

Several of them responded, "Yes."

"Well, let's get it started. Who is it for?". Despite

226

spending nine lost days in a hospital bed, I still was not prepared for what was coming next.

One of my children responded, in a small and trembling voice, "Daddy, it's for you. We're here because you are addicted to pain medications."

I can't fully describe the feeling that I experienced hearing those words. Angry tears instantly welled up in my eyes, as I searched for words to express myself. "Excuse me! How dare you speak to me this way! I have never been addicted to anything in my life. I don't drink or smoke and I've taught you not to do those things either!"

"We know, Daddy, but we've been trying to tell you what's going on. Your disposition and health have changed for the worse and we are all very worried."

The sadness and remorse with which they spoke should have tempered me, but I could not accept what was being said. I was furious! I walked up to each of my children individually and looked them squarely in the eyes. "Look at me. Do you think that I'm addicted to drugs?"

One by one, they all said, "Yes," with tears streaming down their faces.

Finally, I went over to Mike. "You tell me; do you think

I'm addicted to drugs too?"

Mike looked at me squarely, with compassionate firmness. "Brownie, I'm with the family."

My heart dropped and I nearly fell to my knees. I stood in the middle of the room, consumed with fury. I could not speak and no one else spoke either, but the silence was loud and raging.

A few minutes passed, which seemed like a lifetime. Then Serena, who has always been my heartstring and had a great influence over me, broke the silence. "Dad, you don't see that you're addicted because like you say to people all the time, you can't see the picture when you're in the frame. You never had to go out and get the drugs. They were always given to you, so it doesn't seem like an addiction."

Still in shock, I listened to my family's pleas for me to admit what was happening and to seek help. And like almost every intervention I've ever been a part of — when I was on the other side of the intervention — *I was in denial*. "I'm not addicted," I said, just as every addict would most likely say. As did I on that painful night when I was the one who needed the help and support that I had provided for so many others.

After many hours of heart-wrenching pleas and tears and anger, the couple that was there that I didn't recognize walked over to me. One of them spoke and said, "Mr. Brown, your children have paid for you to come to our rehabilitation center for six weeks. We will be back to get you in the morning."

My response was instant. I had no fight left in me and no resistance. If at least one of them had been on my side, I may have stood my ground. However, I was completely defeated, and my words told the story. "No, take me tonight. There is no way that I am going to be here in the morning if you don't."

## *Am I Hallucinating?*

It was a three-hour drive to the center. All the way there I was crying and angrily talking to myself. It was completely surreal. I couldn't believe any of it. *Me, Les Brown, being driven to a drug rehab center?* No! It was unfathomable!

But if you think the intervention was bad, believe me, the real humiliation didn't begin until I arrived at the rehab center. I walked into a strange place that felt cold and uninviting and was asked to remove all my clothes. I

had to take off my belt, shoes, watch — *everything else down to my mickey mouse underwear.* I was then taken to my "room" if you can honestly call it that. It was more like a box. I had the claustrophobic feeling of being inside an oversized coffin. I didn't sleep a wink the entire night. I sat awake in a state of shock, fury, and despair. I just kept thinking to myself, "*What about me makes them think I'm a drug addict?*" Not only was my soul hurting, but my body was hurting as well. I hadn't had any of my pain pills, so my pain
was at its maximum level.

After making it through the first night, it only got worse the next morning when I had to go to the common breakfast area. My humiliation levels were as maxed out as my pain levels. I saw people do double-takes looking at me. I could tell that some of them recognized me. My presence there was surely their entertainment that morning. I overheard a conversation between some of them who were discussing which celebrity I was.

One guy said, "Isn't that Barry White?"

Another one commented, "Looks like Gerald Levert to me."

Then one of the ladies figured it out. "Oh, my goodness! No, I think that's Les Brown!"

Further along in the day, I had to go to a meeting. During the meeting, someone finally dared to walk up to me and ask me if I was Les Brown. When I said, 'Yes,' he said, "Wow, I watch your videos!"

I later learned that one of the symptoms of withdrawal is hallucinations and that some of them literally thought they were only hallucinating that I was there! Even junkies knew that Les Brown didn't belong in a rehab! *(laugh)*

The next day in the group, I listened as people got up and said their names and gave their drug of choice. I heard it all crack, cocaine, heroin, meth, oxy. When it was my turn, I participated with the rest of them. Although I hated being there and suffered extreme humiliation, I never looked down on anyone or tried to close myself off from the other patients. I stood up and told them my name and all the drugs I was taking. After I finished, one of them responded, "Oh, wow! You're on the big horse!" I didn't even know what that meant, but I knew it did not sound good.

As I think back on that experience, it amazes me that even in that state, I was still motivating and inspiring people. Once the residents learned who I was, many of them came to me for advice. They loved talking to me and, even in my weakness, I empowered them. Everything happens for a reason — some we may never understand, but I believe my presence there changed somebody's life.

*Your Heart-Centered desire and HUNGER will always show up in a crisis! Who are you? What do you love to do? What flows out of you naturally, even when in the worst of circumstances? The answer to these questions is key to understanding your purpose and your calling!*

As much as I enjoyed helping the other residents, by the fifth day, I just couldn't take that place anymore. I went into the director's office and said, "Listen to me. There are two types of drug addicts. Some people seek out and buy drugs and those who are prescribed drugs. I've never bought any illegal drugs in my life. I've never gone out to get drugs because of some craving. I'm not a drug addict. These medications for pain were prescribed by my doctor."

He looked at me and said, "Every junkie has a story."

I lost it! "Are you calling me a damned junkie?" I quickly grabbed the telephone that was sitting on his desk and I was prepared to bust him in the head with it!

Fortunately, there was a staff member close by who came up to me and peacefully suggested for me to calm down. Her presence reminded me of something I'd heard many years ago: "It's very easy to get into trouble, but hard to get out of it." Her voice resonated with me and so, instead of using the phone to catch a criminal case, I used it to make a call to Patrick, my second son. I told him, in no uncertain terms, that he needed to come and get me from that place IMMEDIATELY.

He tried to reason with me and said, "Daddy, we paid a a lot of money for you to be there for six weeks."

My mind was made up and I was irate. I screamed at him, "I don't care about any of that! Come and get me now or I'll leave here walking!"

He knew I was serious. I probably would have frozen stiff in the cold winter night if I had walked. But I was getting out of that place one way or another, so he agreed to pick me up as soon as possible.

On the three-hour drive back, he and I argued the entire time. I know he was worried about what would happen to me if I returned home and continued to use the drugs. Patrick insisted that I was always determined to get my way. He tried to urge me to look at what it was costing me. I could understand his point of view, but I let him know that I couldn't get off the medications in that environment. I'd have to do it on my own.

## *Give Me Freedom Or Give Me Death!*

During my time at rehab, I learned a lot about the drugs that I was taking. It was the other residents who educated me about withdrawal and drug interactions and the recovery process. Although I left there still in denial about being an addict, I was at least educated enough to know what to look for. It didn't take long for the scales to finally fall off my eyes once I was home. I was on a buffer drug while at the rehab. When I returned home, I was not taking it any longer and my body began to crave the painkillers. That is when it finally hit me — *I was indeed an addict!*

When I realized that I truly was battling addiction, I did my research to determine the best way to win the fight. I went to a variety of counselors, including a psychiatrist and psychologist. I also went to various medical doctors and talked with them about how I should proceed. Once I found a doctor that I felt comfortable with, we talked about options for getting off the prescription painkillers. She recommended that I take a medication called Suboxone to help wean me off. I remembered the name of the medication she suggested from one of the group meetings at the rehab center. One of the residents had mentioned that he was in the process of trying to get off it!

Thinking of his story, I asked the doctor if the medication she was recommending was an addictive substance. She confirmed that it was and informed me that I would need to take it for one to two years to safely and effectively get off the painkillers. I was blown away and dumbfounded! Feeling confused, I asked her, "So your plan is to take me off the addictive drugs that I am on now and replace them with another addictive drug?" When she again confirmed my fears, I emphatically let her know that there was no way

I was going to take another addictive pill. I also informed her that I would no longer be using her services and that I would stop using the drugs on my own!

Of course, she wanted to argue with me. She told me that the likelihood of me being able to kick the addiction on my own was nearly impossible, considering my age. She informed me that if I were in my twenties or even my thirties, there would be a slight increase in my chances to wean myself away from the painkillers. However, she believed that at my age, there was just no way I could do it without using some type of buffer drugs to help with the process. In her professional opinion, the symptoms of withdrawal would most likely kill me.

At that point, nothing was going to convince me otherwise. As I was leaving her office, I made this declaration to her, "That's fine. I'd rather die than stay addicted to something I never wanted to begin with!" It was hard to get to the place of acceptance concerning my drug addiction. But once I accepted it, I was HUNGRY to be free of it and nothing would stop me, not even the threat of death!

My loved ones were up in arms about my choice to quit cold turkey. I feel terrible for what I put them through. I can't imagine what it was like for them. After I finally got off the drugs, I found pills hidden *everywhere*.

They were in my socks, the cushions of the couch, in drawers, and so many other places! I remember finding some hidden pills one day after my addiction ended and asking, "Who put these here?" My kids responded, "YOU, 'Mr. I'm not an addict!'"

My children were trying to save my life, but my arrogance and ignorance were making me deaf to their pleas. Then when I finally accepted my addiction, they had to face the fear that I might kill myself through withdrawal! That had to be horrifying for them and I will never be able to accurately express my remorse and regret. *Please forgive me.*

## **<u>The Process</u>**

Although I do not agree with the use of addictive medications to wean patients from painkillers, I do agree with part of the doctor's advice — *I would not recommend that anyone quit a drug addiction cold turkey!* I did not know what I was signing up for when I made that choice and I would never suggest that someone take the route that I took. When your body is chemically dependent, denying yourself the chemicals can be just as life-threatening as using them. Quit by all means! But I suggest finding safe, non-addictive treatments that can help ensure you survive!

*Although I don't regret my decision to quit cold turkey, and it was admittedly worth everything I suffered to be free today, what I went through during the detoxification process was worse than a living hell! I will never be able to find the words to accurately describe it, but I will do my best to paint a picture for you.*

It began with dry heaving. If you've ever heard a cat trying to cough up a hairball, that is the sound that I made all day long. When I wasn't dry heaving, I was vomiting. For nearly two months, I vomited between twenty-five to thirty times a day. The vomiting and heaving caused intense pain in my throat and life-threatening dehydration because I couldn't even keep water down. Anything that came near my lips caused me to vomit. And when there was nothing in my stomach to throw up, my intestines themselves tried to come out.

On top of the vomiting, I was sweating profusely all the time. I would go from an extremely hot sweat to an extreme cold sweat as the chemicals were vengefully leaving my body. There were times that I would begin to violently shake and in between the shakes, there were tremors — like earthquakes and aftershocks. My mood was completely altered and I hallucinated at times. I recall "seeing" giraffes running through the living room. I don't know why my mind chose to see giraffes — maybe because I felt like I was in a jungle trying to escape a predator!

I was in intense pain constantly, so much pain that I would sometimes pass out. The pain of withdrawal far surpassed the pain that I initially started taking the painkillers for. The cancer pain, the sciatica pain, and the other pain types, which I had been dealing with that led to the drugs being prescribed in the first place, were all localized. Those pains were excruciating, but they showed mercy by remaining in the one area of the body that was targeted. The pain of withdrawal was like a ruthless mercenary compared to the other pain I had experienced. It was unrelenting torture that consumed every part of my body and my soul.

All my fluid levels and electrolytes were thrown completely off balance. On several occasions, I had to be rushed to urgent care where I was given fluids intravenously. On my sixth trip to the ER, I recall overhearing one of the nurses say, "He's not going to make it cold turkey. He's gonna have to take a buffer drug!"

I can't say that I blame her or anyone who didn't believe that I could make it. Anyone watching what I was going through would have thought the same.

By that time in my life, my biological mother, my adoptive mother, my best friend, Bou, and my nephew, Wes Jr., had all died. I remember the days that I began doing something that I had never done in all the difficult situations in my life — *I called out to them for help!* I believe in angels, so I called on them all!

Of course, I don't remember my exact words, but I screamed out something like this: "Mother who gave me life, I've never asked you for anything, but I know you hear me, Mother who gave me love, I know you're gone, but I believe you're watching me and I need you. Bou, Wes Jr., please help me! Please hear me and help me get through this! I need you all right now!!! PLEASE HELP ME!" I begged GOD and my heavenly family for help, and I believe that they all heard me and they all helped me.

It seemed like the detoxification process would never end, but eventually, it did. I knew that it was over the day I finally woke up without dry heaving. I wasn't sweating anymore. I could eat without vomiting and I was no longer trembling. That was one of the best moments of my life, knowing that I had made it through to the other side of withdrawal. The detox only lasted eight weeks, but it felt more like eight years. Nonetheless, it was over. I was free. I had won.

Even with all that I've shared about this process, I will never be able to accurately describe to you what it was like to go through that period. Although I have never experienced anything as painful or intense as those sixty days, I am living proof that *there is nothing as powerful as a made-up mind!* My children, my counselor, and my psychiatrist were all in shock that I was able to go cold turkey, ridding my body of prescription painkillers — but I wasn't. I was **HUNGRY** and I knew I would win!

# You've Got to be HUNGRY

When you have a *Heart-Centered, Unshakeable Faith,* compounded with *NOW Urgency* that is *Growing Continuously* with the right *Relationship Impact* and an unequivocal *YES LORD!* Your chances of Winning will be Improved Exponentially—

**The Conclusion: I Have Kobe Power**

# The Conclusion

# I Have Kobe Power!

## The HUNGER to Do It

# The Greatness Within to Win

## A Race to the Moon

In 1961, during a period that is referred to as *"The Space Race,"* President John F. Kennedy met with his cabinet and said, "We're going to beat Russia to the moon." He looked at the most brilliant German scientist of the day, Wernher von Braun, and asked him what it would take to get to the moon before the projected Russian target date. Everyone in the room sat poised in front of their typewriters or with pens in hand, ready to listen to a long lecture and take copious notes.

When Wernher opened his mouth to answer the President's question, he spoke just five short and simple words. President Kennedy sat waiting for him to say more, as did everyone else in the room. As the silence lingered on, the room first grew tense and then calm as von Braun just sat there and let those five famous words sink into the atmosphere.

Eventually, those five words spoke with the force of a million. On May 25, 1961, President Kennedy, embracing the weight and gravity of those five words even at the risk of global embarrassment, responded with this declaration: "That's it. We're going to the moon! Call a press conference to announce it. We are going to the moon within ten years!" He was confident that the U.S. could and would beat its Cold War rival, Russia, in landing a man on the moon!

*Those five words* were all it took to get us to the moon. Without any logistical plan, not knowing the "how-to" or even what it would cost, **the force of those five words, and the power of the message they delivered, GUARANTEED** a mission accomplished. On that day, JFK's unshakeable faith began the mission with his bold press conference announcement. Just eight years later, on July 20, 1969, an American astronaut planted the U.S. flag on the moon, far ahead of our Cold War rival, Russia. We had won the space race to the moon. Our faith was realized, our greatness and superiority as a nation established; the mission was successfully completed.

*I'm sure you're itching to know just what those five simple, yet mighty words were...*

# THE

# WILL

# TO

# DO

# IT

All it took to get U.S. astronauts to the moon was ***the will to do it!*** Should any goal or dream seem too far-fetched or impossible for you to accomplish, knowing what you know about what has already been achieved? *The will to do it* is mighty. A ***Heart-Centered***, gut-based, spirit-driven desire is unstoppable!

However, I'd like to make a slight tweak to those five famous words. To accomplish what seems improbable or maybe even impossible, for you to beat your enemies in your own "race to space", to overcome odds that are stacked against you, to defeat tragedy, setbacks, and losses, to face down your fears and go after your dreams, to embrace your greatness and live a life that will outlive you, it takes only one thing: ***THE HUNGER TO DO IT!***

## THE HUNGER to Do It!

The story that I shared about my drug addiction and how I overcame it was not only the hardest story to tell, it was also the hardest to live through. Without ***the HUNGER to do it,*** I never would have made it through that situation. I am fortunate to have had the support system that I did at the time. However, I would be remiss if I did not discuss one of my biggest sources of strength, which came from an unexpected place. It was the memory of a ten-year-old boy named Kobe.

Several years prior to the addiction episode, I was staying with one of my mentees. We were conducting a workshop in his area. That night when I was trying to rest at his home, I kept hearing a repetitive sound that made it impossible to sleep. *Bam! Bam! Bam!*

Initially, I tried to ignore it, but it got to the point that I wondered if I should be alarmed because I didn't know what was happening! After quite some time of enduring the sound, I couldn't take it any longer, so I went to inquire about it. "What is that loud hammering sound that I keep hearing?" I asked.

His response was surprising. "Wow, I guess we don't even notice it anymore. My son, Kobe, was diagnosed with a rare condition in his intestines when he was very young. It is very uncomfortable and causes him a lot of pain throughout the day. At night, he hits his punching bag as much as he needs to, to release his frustrations."

After learning what was producing the sound, I loved hearing it. Kobe's punches soothed me to sleep that night like white noise.

## *You've Got to be HUNGRY*

During the detox process, there was never a moment that I doubted I would beat the drug addiction. There was never a moment that I regretted my decision to go cold turkey. However, there were plenty of moments that I didn't know *how* I was going to make it through the process. It was in those moments that I had to reach deep inside of myself and find inspiration from somewhere, something that would fuel my HUNGER.

When I was going through the worst parts of the withdrawal process, I remembered the sound of Kobe punching the frustration of his pain away — over and over again — on his punching bag. I thought about that soothing sound and said to myself, *"If a ten-year-old boy can find a way to release his pain, without an abusive substance, certainly a man in his seventies can do the same."*

Whenever the cravings came, I would say to myself, *"I am more than a conqueror; I have Kobe power! I'm more than a conqueror; I have Kobe power!"*

When I looked in the mirror and didn't recognize myself. I said, *"I am more than a conqueror; I have Kobe power!"*

When the doctors or my family would try to get me to

take buffer drugs to help with the process, I remembered the sound of Kobe punching that bag and I said to myself, *"I am more than a conqueror; I have Kobe power!"*

In every difficult moment, as often as I needed to, I said those words to myself, ***"I am more than a conqueror. I have Kobe power!"***

The HUNGER of that ten-year-old boy to live a life free of painkillers and to beat what was trying to beat him inspired me. In my darkest hour, it reminded me of the unstoppable force of ***HUNGER — the greatest power given to humanity.*** I thought of all that I'd taught over the years and what it would take to both live and die on my terms. We all must die one day, but I made a firm decision that neither drug addiction nor withdrawal was going to be the 'period' on my life story!

No matter what you are going through in your life right now or no matter what you will go through, you too are more than a conqueror! You have the power within yourself to overcome any obstacle, but your faith must be unshakable, and your HUNGER unrelenting! When you are facing challenges, tap into your HUNGER to win, *and you will!*

Like Kobe, you will overcome incredible odds and be

empowered to take control over whatever life throws at you. If you are addicted to drugs, alcohol or a toxic relationship, if you are experiencing debilitating pain, if you are facing a life-threatening illness — *anything that does not represent the greatness within you* — **I'm here to tell you, you can beat it; you can win!**

Pray, scream, cry — *hit a punching bag repeatedly in the middle of the night so often that it becomes like white noise!* Do whatever you need to do, but don't retreat! I'm here to tell you, GOD will dispatch angels to pull you through! You can get through this! You are stronger than your circumstances, but **You've Got to Be HUNGRY** to win!

No matter what comes your way, honor yourself. Keep your commitment to your commitment. Keep affirming to yourself that you are more than a conqueror! Say to yourself, "**No matter how bad it is or how bad it gets, I'm going to make it! I have already WON!**"

You see, what you need to understand is this: It is not a question of whether you are going to win or lose. Your HUNGER declares you the winner, as soon as it shows up! **HUNGER almost guarantees your win**. From the moment:

- ✓  You make a *Heart-Centered* commitment

- ✓  When you stand firm with *Unshakeable Faith*

- ✓  When you operate with a sense of *NOW Urgency*

- ✓  When you are determined to *Grow Continuously*

- ✓  When you value *Relationship Impact* around you

- ✓  When you say an unequivocal *YES LORD* in your soul


*YOU HAVE ALREADY WON! Baby, every fight is fixed from that point forward! No matter what the scoreboard shows at certain points during the match, **you will be declared the undefeated champion of your own destiny!!!***


So, what did it take to get to the moon before the Russians? **The HUNGER to Do It.** What will it take for YOU to become the next greatest version of yourself and live out every principle in this book? That's right! **The HUNGER to Do It!** No matter what it is that you want to achieve after today, all you need is *THE HUNGER TO DO IT!*

# You've Got to be HUNGRY

What will it take for you to rebuild your sense of self and defeat the negative mentality that has held you back?
*The HUNGER to Do It!*

What will it take for you to overcome setbacks, such as divorce, monetary loss or a terminal medical diagnosis?
*The HUNGER to Do It!*

What will it take for you to end those toxic relationships that have been sucking the life out of you for years?
*The HUNGER to Do It!*

What will it take for you to be able to walk away from a job that makes you miserable and tap into your true passion?
*The HUNGER to Do It!*

What will it take for you to discover your purpose and calling and embrace your undeniable greatness?
*The HUNGER to Do It!*

What will it take for you to go after your BIG dream and forget about the odds and naysayers?

*The HUNGER to Do It!*

What will it take for you to face down your fears and embrace what is rightfully yours?

*The HUNGER to Do It!*

What will it take for you to throw away every excuse, stop procrastinating and live a life that will out-live you?

*The HUNGER to Do It!*

I don't know you, but here's what I know about you – **You Have Greatness Within You!** Here's what I also know, you must **know your dream is possible** and **be Relentless and Unstoppable** to bring that greatness out and make it count! When you are pursuing your destiny and your purpose, you must be just like the bumblebee who doesn't know he isn't supposed to be able to fly. You don't know what your limitations are, so act like you don't have any and soar high! It's MORE than possible, but...

## You've Got to Be HUNGRY!

## If You Want It Bad Enough

*"If you want a thing bad enough to go out and fight for it,*

*to work day and night for it,*

*to give up your time, your peace, and your sleep for*

*it, if all that you dream and scheme is about it,*

*and life seems useless and worthless without it,*

*if you gladly sweat for it, and fret for it, and plan for it,*

*and lose all your terror of the opposition for it,*

*if you simply go after that thing that you want*

*with all of your capacity, strength and sagacity,*

*faith, hope and confidence, and stern*

*pertinacity, if neither cold, poverty, famine, nor*

*gout, sickness nor pain, of body and brain,*

*can keep you away from the thing that you*

*want, if dogged and grim you beseech and*

*beset it, with the help of God, you will surely*

*get it!"*

*~by Berton Braley~*

*In the loving memory of the woman who gave me Love, Ms. Mamie Brown.*

## END NOTES

1.  1 Corinthians 3:16 (KJV)

2.  Psalm 37:4 (KJV, authors' paraphrase)

3.  Matthew 6:21 (NKJV)

4.  Proverbs 3:5 (KJV)

5.  Joshua 24:15 (KJV)

6.  Proverbs 23:7 (KJV)

7.  William Shatner, "You'll Have Time," by Ben Folds, Benjamin Scott Folds, and William Shatner, track 3 on *Has Been*, Shout! Factory, 2004.

8.  "World Health Organization: Suicide across the world (2016)," https://www.who.int/mental_health/prevention/s uicide/suicideprevent/en/ (accessed February 11, 2020).

# Afterword

My father, Les Brown, who has been named one of the top five speakers in the world, is well-known for sharing hundreds of soul-stirring, thought-provoking quotes. One of his top favorites simply says, "Life is a fight for territory and once you stop fighting for what you want what you don't want will automatically take over!" One of the key factors in the fight for our heart's desire is the amount of hunger that we have deep inside of us, which serves as an inner fuel to propel us forward beyond the seen and unforeseen obstacles that we must conquer along our journey.

But what is hunger? According to one definition, hunger is a powerful desire or craving for something. It is when one's body and/or mind is consumed with the desire to secure something that will provide a sense of satisfaction, relief or fulfillment. Hunger is a drive to live a life greater than yourself. It begins with you then spreads out beyond you to those that resonate with your mission. Your hunger first impacts those in your inner circle, then it touches your community. If you are blessed, it then multiplies out into the world.

Referred to as a living legend, Les Brown has lived by this 'hunger philosophy' throughout his lifetime. It was my grandmother, Ms. Mamie Brown, that initially ignited his burning desire, at a very impressionable age. My grandmother sacrificed everything to adopt my dad and his siblings and to provide them with a loving and safe home. He observed how much she gave of herself. It sparked a hunger for a better life within him and a desire for my grandmother to have more of the finer things that life had to offer!

As my dad grew into a young man his hunger was fueled to burn even hotter, by his childhood mentor, Mr. Leroy Washington. Searching and reaching out for more ways to expand his hidden talents and potential was second nature for my dad. In the midst of him exploring life, he realized that he was destined to impart to others what was deposited in him. This is when the vision of becoming the world's leading transformational voice was established!

**Sometimes the Road is Rough**

Know that there is always a sacrifice that must be made when you or someone you love has been given a vision greater than self to impact the world as an agent of change, in a powerful and uplifting way. However, through it all, may we continue to stand and press forward. May we remember that we are descendants of the ones who did not give up and fought hard so that we could live the life that we are now graciously living. The Brown family matriarch, Ms. Mamie Brown, showed us the way. She exemplified, in her granted years here on this earth, the ability to always *dance through life and make a way out of no way.*

Affectionately known as, *Mamie Brown's Baby Boy,* Les Brown is the second generation of a walking demonstration of Hunger Personified. He has defied the odds time and time again. He has risen above physical challenges, setbacks, deaths, disappointments, rejections and heartaches countless times. Yet he still continues to stand and educate, motivate and empower people from all walks of life all around the world, when most people would have crumbled up and given out. Les continues to snatch victory from the jaws of defeat and *call forth those things that be not as though they were.*

## *You've Got to be HUNGRY*

Whatever you may be facing in your own reality, just know that you have the power to *Live Your Dreams* and *It's Not Over Until You Win!* If Les Brown can make it from the slums of Liberty City in Miami, Florida to gracing stages across the planet as a first-class professional speaker, then you can create a life that will make you say, "Wow, I LOVE MY LIFE!"

This body of work was designed to move you into your next level of greatness and to open you up to unimaginable possibilities... *with a sense of urgency.* So, go ahead and dive back in and get filled up with all the knowledge, wisdom, truths, information and insights that your hungry mind can stand. Be sure to become a part of the *You've got to Be HUNGRY* online community by visiting *www.iamhugrylesbrown.com* or *scanning the QR code* in the front of the book. Apply these principles and methods to your own life and prepare for the rest of your life to be the best of your life. In the meantime, whatever

you do, always remember and never forget **YOU'VE GOT**

**TO BE HUNGRY!**


Dr. Ona Love Brown

Corporate Trainer/The Message Midwife/Author/Brand

Builder and Les Brown's Baby Girl!  :-)

Onabrown.com

# About the Author

As one of the world's most renowned motivational speakers, Les Brown is a dynamic personality and highly-sought-after resource in business and professional circles for Fortune 500 CEOs, small business owners, non-profit and community leaders from all sectors of society looking to expand opportunity. For five decades he has not only studied the science of achievement, he's mastered it by interviewing thousands of successful business leaders and collaborating with them in the boardroom, translating theory into bottom-line results for his clients.

As a premier Keynote Speaker and leading authority on achievement for audiences as large as 80,000 – Les Brown energizes people to meet the challenges of the world around them. He skillfully weaves his compelling life story into the fabric of our daily lives. The thread is forever strengthened, touting why you can't afford to be complacent and to aim high, achieve and actively make an impact on the world.

Les Brown never tires of using his energies to transform the world, well beyond the podium and public appearances, meshing traditional and social media to empower his audiences. Hundreds of thousands are watching and interacting with him on YouTube and Facebook. He has a keen way of turning what he touches into gold. Over 20 years ago, he won a Chicago-area Emmy® for his unsurpassed fundraising pledge drive for the Public Broadcasting System. Followed by several bestselling books and hosting popular national talk shows on television and radio.

Addressing audiences from Denmark to Dubai, Canada to the Caribbean, Les Brown is invited back again and again for his powerful message and the ability to connect deeply with people from all walks of life. It isn't just his great smile and his way with words that motivates people to take action like never before; when people face roadblocks or adversity it is the depth of his knowledge on achievement that creates lasting results.

Les Brown's straight-from-the-heart, passion and high-energy motivates audiences to step beyond their limitations and into their greatness in many ways. Over the past two decades, Les has expanded his role from keynote speaker to Master Trainer, creating the kind of workshop learning experience that got him committed to personal and professional development many years earlier. His charisma, warmth and humor have transformed ordinary people into extraordinary achievers by using his own life, and his in-depth study of others' challenges, to build an understanding of what works, what doesn't work, and why.

Revered as an icon by his colleagues, Brown received the much-coveted National Speakers Association Council of Peers Award of Excellence (CPAE), and ultimately, its most prestigious Golden Gavel Award for achievement and leadership in communication. Toastmasters International also voted him one of the Top Five Outstanding Speakers. Worldwide. Legions of followers flock to stadiums and arenas to hear a man who never stops believing that with proper guidance and training you can achieve anything you desire in life.

A stumbling block in elementary school was when he was mistakenly declared, "educable mentally retarded," teachers did not recognize the true potential of little Les Brown. However, he used determination, persistence and belief in his ability to go beyond being a sanitation worker to unleash a course of amazing achievements including broadcast station manager, political commentator and multi-term state representative in Ohio.

Les Brown is committed to motivating and training today's generation to be achievers and leaders as he introduces new audiences every day to *It's Not Over Until You Win, Up Thoughts for Down Times* and *Fight for Your Dream*. Les Brown's audio series, "Choosing Your Future," remains his all-time bestseller for its acclaimed impact worldwide.

In business, as in real life, there are always going to be

ups and downs. However, where there is a will, there is always a way to achieve amazing results for your organization when Les Brown fills the room with his high-impact, customized message and standing ovation performance!

# *Your Dream is POSSIBLE!*

Made in the USA
Monee, IL
30 March 2020

24194224R00149